SPORTING SPITE!

Rebels and Rebellion in World Sport

 Evening Standard Sports Writers

WARD LOCK

First published in 1991 by Ward Lock

Villiers House, 41–47 Strand,
London WC2N 5JE, England

A Cassell imprint

ISBN 0–7063–7078–3

Typeset by Litho Link Limited, Welshpool Powys.
Printed and bound in Great Britain by
Hartnolls Limited, Bodmin

Front top. Although John McEnroe had assured the world he
could now cope with disputed calls, he still launched a
tirade against a line judge during his defeat by Stefann
Edberg at Wimbledon 1991.

Front below. At a time when crowd control and
behaviour had improved in the British game, soccer again
showed its unsavoury side with a bout of arguing and fighting
between the players of Arsenal and Manchester United in
October 1990.

CONTENTS

CONTRIBUTORS

Michael Herd is Assistant Editor and Head of Sport at the Evening Standard. An award-winning writer, he has covered Olympic and Commonwealth Games and a string of World Championship boxing matches including the "Rumble in the Jungle" between Muhammed Ali and George Foreman. He has been the Standard's Sports Editor, News Editor and Assistant Editor (news), and acted as Editor of the Evening News when it returned briefly in the 1980's. During a five-year spell away from Fleet Street, he was Editor-in-Chief of a provincial group with 23 titles.

Neil Allen writes on Athletics and Boxing for the Evening Standard. In a career of over 30 years as a sports writer with the Standard and The Times, he has won a British Press Award and has been President of the International Athletic Writers Group.

Peter Blackman has been tennis correspondent of the Evening Standard since 1983 and has covered all the major tournaments around the world in that time. He has strong views on the overpayment of players and the power they exert, and on the lack of depth on the women's tour. Before switching to tennis he worked for 18 years as a soccer reporter, travelling extensively in Europe with the successful English clubs.

Mick Dennis is the Evening Standard's Deputy Sports Editor. Born in in West London he began his career with the Eastern Daily Press in Norwich before returning to the capital to work for the The Sun and The Daily Telegraph.

Chris Jones has been the rugby correspondent of the Evening Standard since 1986. He had previously covered the sport for the Western Mail in Cardiff and for Extel, a national sports agency. He has reported tours in South Africa, Australia, New Zealand and Argentina.

Renton Laidlaw is the most travelled golf writer in the world. Each year, as the Evening Standard's golf correspondent – a post he has held since 1973, he covers over 40 events in America, Australia, South Africa and Europe.

He spends a total of three weeks a year at 35,000 feet commuting between tournaments, making an average 100 flights every 12 months. He also works for television and radio.

Christopher Poole has been racing correspondent of the Evening Standard for over 20 years, has made over 2000 broadcasts for BBC World Service Radio and written or edited fourteen books devoted to the Turf. He is former holder of the coveted Derby Award as racing journalist of the year.

David Smith joined the Evening Standard in 1980 after spells with local papers in Hertfordshire and the specialist publication, Motoring News. As a member of the Standard's sports writing team he covers motor racing, football, boxing, golf and tennis; he has raced in several types of racing car and partnered leading driver, Roger Clark in the Autoglass Tour of Britain.

John Thicknesse joined the Evening Standard as cricket correspondent in 1967 after periods with the Daily Express and Daily and Sunday Telegraphs. He has reported on 225 Test Matches, an unknown number of one-day internationals and many overseas tours.

Garth Crooks achieved considerable success as a goalscorer with Stoke City, Tottenham Hotspur and Charlton. His ability to discuss the deeper elements of professional sport led him to become Chairman of the footballer's union, the PFA, and regularly voice his views on radio and television.

Caroline Searle is Press Officer of the British Olympic Association and has been close to developments in international sports organisation. From this position she has a wide view of several sports, from the grass-roots to the superstars.

INTRODUCTION

Michael Herd

One week-end, as rugby union's 1991 World Cup headed for the final at Twickenham and motor-racing's world championship reached a pulsating climax in Tokyo, there were several illustrations of a decline in sporting behaviour. They were prime examples of what can be termed Sporting Spite.

Serge Blanco, the most capped player in rugby history, the much revered captain of France, was playing his final international before his home crowd in the Parc des Princes, Paris. The game had hardly started when Blanco knocked out England winger Nigel Heslop with a sweeping right hand punch. Other Frenchmen were raining blows on the diminutive Englishman and he was unconscious before he hit the ground.

On the other side of the world in Japan, the brilliant Brazilian driver, Ayrton Senna, had clinched his third world championship and provided further evidence that he was on the threshold of becoming the world's most successful driver. He chose Tokyo to confess that a year previously, ignoring risks to life and limb, he had deliberately driven into the car of arch-rival Alain Prost causing the pair to crash. In doing so, Senna had clinched the world championship.

Back in Paris, French coach Daniel Dubroca, desperately disappointed at the defeat by England, had pinned referee David Bishop by the lapels of his jersey and screamed one word repeatedly in English. 'Cheat!' he cried. Afterwards the Frenchman vehemently denied he had attacked the referee. Oui, he said, he had made a point of meeting the referee in the tunnel as the players left the field. Non, he had not attacked Bishop. The meeting was to thank the New Zealander for refereeing the quarter-final, to offer him fraternal greetings and, presumably, to kiss him on each cheek. Subsequently, as the weight of evidence grew against him, Dubroca confessed that, carried away by the passion of the moment, he had indeed accused the innocent official of being a cheat. A few days later he resigned. It was a sorry end to what had been a distinguished career.

In the same match, another French player, Pascal Ondarts, twice tried to strike the referee, the first time in full view of the packed stadium and, indeed, of the rest of the rugby world watching on television. Meanwhile, on the same day over in Dublin the match between Ireland and Australia had barely started before players were at each other's throats, fists flying as forwards attempted to establish superiority over one another. There were accusations of spitting and other assaults, all of which drew a storm of protest, followed by demands for action, as the World Cup was played out.

In his foolishness, Russell Thomas, Chairman of the World Cup Organising Committee, declared that no action was to be taken. Thomas said, defensively, that the rest of us could accuse him of brushing the brutality under the carpet but the matter was closed. There was an uncomfortable feeling that French coach Dubroca, referee Bishop and Thomas has acted like the monkeys who had spoken, heard and seen no evil.

All in all, it was not a good week-end for sport. If there had been any doubts before, there was none afterwards. What we had seen and heard was yet more evidence that the world of sport is becoming more vociferously vicious and unmistakably, unacceptably physical. There were no doubts then and there is none now that an increase in sporting spite is testament to a decline in sporting behaviour. There have been too many such week-ends for comfort.

We are entitled to ask in anger what on earth is happening to sport? There was a time when we watched in awe, respect and pleasure, those who produced winning performances. On and off the field of play, sportsmen and women were honest, sincere, competent and determined but not ruthless.

Sport was used a yardstick for civilised behaviour. Cricket was a synonym for all that was true and honest. A good fellow could be relied to play a straight bat. Conduct unbecoming simply wasn't cricket. When you played the game you were doing the right thing.

Somewhere along the way, however, sport has been permitted, even encouraged, to change. Does anybody have any doubts that today it is being used to encourage personal and group vanities, hatred for rivals and, as Aldous Huxley once said, to create an intolerant esprit de corps and contempt for people who are beyond an arbitrarily selected pale.

Football has its professional foul, cricket has sledging and racist taunts, tennis has John McEnroe and athletics has Ben Johnson. Even golf, the most gentlemanly and honourable of pursuits, has been marred by the conduct of spectators, particularly at recent Ryder Cup matches between Europe and the United States.

Rugby's World Cup was intended to be a celebration of a sport unknown in many parts of the world. A way to spread the gospel. Instead, on the week-end to which I have referred, what the public witnessed were scenes that, outside the local pub, would have led to overnight confinement in the 'nick' and subsequent appearances in court.

Of course, rugby has never been a game for softies. It is a contact sport between men who ruck and maul and scrum down. Even the unfortunate

Nigel Heslop agrees that an occasional smack is within the spirit of the game. And smacks they get. But to use that as an excuse for violence on the field is to miss the point.

Rob Andrew of Wasps played against the French. He has won more caps than any England fly-half in history and played an essential role in England's World Cup performances. He puts it this way. 'The more you play, the more caps you have, the harder it gets because more people are trying to knock your block off. I know that if I end up on the floor, even if it's well away from the ball someone is going to come along and boot me. You know it's going to happen. You know that if you get caught in there, someone is going to throw a punch. The thing is you get 'nutters' playing. If they don't get sorted out, they keep doing it. And these 'nutters' can be very subtle.'

Isn't it time to reflect on what has happened to sport? I suggest we have allowed ourselves to confuse the pursuit of sporting excellence with the scramble for money or political prestige. And as a result too many of us today condone what seems to be an irresistible compulsion for participants to behave badly. Let there be no doubt, though, that whatever external pressures exist, at the end of the day each participant is able to act according to his own moral values.

As fists and four-letter words fly, is sport a mirror of our society in which, with arrogance and disdain, rules are bent so that Authority is tested? Do we all see what we can get away with on the field of play and off it? Perhaps E M Forster was correct when he wrote that it is international sport that has helped to kick the world downhill?

All things considered, this is the appropriate time for sport's ruling bodies to declare enough is enough. How much violence will be tolerated before rugby and other sports act to replace anarchy with authority? At the very moment that baseness seems to have become a daily feature of our sporting lives, is there a way back to a golden age, to the Corinthian era? Some will say that sport should not look over its shoulder while the rest of the world makes what is declared as progress. But surely we want to return to the good old days?

So what is the solution? Does it lie with the players or the administrators or the spectators? Does it lie with all of us? The Evening Standard's team of writers is not alone in feeling that action is required. There is a powerful group, led by the Duke of Edinburgh, who, emphatically, agree. Not long before the incidents which marred the France-England rugby match (I hesitate to call it a game!) Prince Philip, claiming that the moral values of sport has reached an all-time low, led a Central Council of Physical Recreation initiative upholding the virtues of playing the game. The result was Fair Play in Sport, a charter of conduct for those involved in sport.

The ethos of courage, athleticism, resoluteness and honour have gone, says the charter, and been replaced by standards of behaviour by competitors, spectators and commentators so unacceptable that they threaten to undermine the very purpose of sport.

Last year the Duke hosted a unique conference at Windsor Castle. It was attended by some of the most famous figures in British sport in an attempt to achieve a renaissance of ethical principles. Sebastian Coe and Mary Peters, both Olympic gold medallists, were there. So were Colin Cowdrey, chairman of the International Cricket Conference, Sports Minister Robert Atkins, Peter Coni, chairman of Henley Royal Regatta, and Garth Crooks, a former chairman of the Professional Footballer's Association.

The conference was held at the suggestion of the Duke who, for years, has said that participation in the right spirit is the most important part of sport. Everything else is a bonus. Like you and I, he knows of the baleful effect on the younger generation of frequent examples of serious misconduct and malpractice in popular spectator sports.

He is aware that young people learn by precept and example. They are influenced by the behaviour of their heroes in their favourite sports. When soccer players cavort round the field punching the air to celebrate a goal, when Paul Gascoigne commits a brutal foul in an FA Cup Final, we know from experience that it will not be long before they are mimicked by worshipping hordes.

The outcome of the Duke of Edinburgh's initiative was A Charter of Conduct for all those involved in sport and physical recreation. The charter set out terms with which no-one can disagree.

In general it declared:

GOVERNING BODIES

1. Must ensure that their rules are fair, thoroughly understood by competitors and officials and properly enforced
2. Must make every effort to ensure that the rules are applied consistently and with absolute impartiality
3. Must make every effort to impress upon participants and officials the absolute need to maintain the highest standards of sportsmanship in the organisation and practice of their sport.

COACHES.

1. Must insist that competitors understand and abide by the principles of good sportsmanship
2. Must not countenance the use of drugs by competitors
3. Must never employ methods or practices that might involve risks to the long-term health or physical development of their charges
4. Must not attempt to manipulate the rules to the advantage of their charges.

COMPETITORS.

1. Must bide by both the laws and the spirit of their sport
2. Must accept the decision of umpires and referees without question or protestation
3. Must not cheat and in particular must not attempt to improve their performance by the use of drugs
4. Must exercise self-control at all times
5. Must accept success and failure, victory and defeat with good grace and without excessive display of emotion
6. Must treat their opponents and fellow participants with due respect at all times.

SPONSORS AND PROMOTERS.

1. Must not seek improperly to influence the outcome of non-professional competitions by financial inducements
2. Must understand and agree that the administration, operation and arrangements for the conduct of competitioned and events are the exclusive responsibility of the governing bodies.

The charter pointed out, with good reason, the particularly vital role played by the media. Newspapers—and television and radio—were urged, in keeping with the Code of Practice agreed by editors of national papers, to maintain the highest standards of responsible journalism in the reporting of sport and in comments on sporting personalities. No less than 70 governing bodies of sport—from the Football Association to the Salmon and Trout Association—endorsed the charter.

But how effective will it be? How many governing bodies will reveal an attitude of laissez faire? How many men and women within sport will pay no more than lip service to the charter? How many will give fair play a fair crack of the whip? But don't you agree that the worst thing of all is to do nothing. After all, we want to save sport for our children rather than have to save our children from sport.

ATHLETICS

Neil Allen

Seoul, South Korea, the Olympic Games of 1988 and the thoughts of American sprinter Carl Lewis, the defending champion, as he goes to his blocks for the start of the 100 metres final.

'Ben Johnson hardly looked at me. I noticed that his eyes were very yellow. A sign of steroid use.

'Ben looked like a weight lifter and I was used to that by now . . but those yellow eyes . . . I couldn't stop thinking about those yellow eyes. That bastard did it again, I said to myself.'

This was certainly the most dramatic moment in all the summer Olympic Games I have covered since Melbourne, 1956, arguably the biggest 'story' since a Greek shepherd named Spiridon Louis won the marathon in Athens in 1896 or Italy's Pietri Dorando, in the same event in London in 1908, was disqualified for having been given assistance across the finishing line. The spite that Lewis, the defending champion from 1980, felt towards his Canadian rival was to be totally justified just a few hours later when bounding Ben, declared the winner of the gold medal in the world record time of 9.79 sec., was found guilty of cheating, positive in a test of his urine, of drug-taking.

As Johnson wept guilty tears, though it would be many months before he would admit that he had broken the rules, track and field athletics shook from the shock and then came to its senses.

As we waited in Seoul the morning after Johnson had fled home, at an emotional Canadian team press conference, I talked with an old friend Robert Pariente, Editor in Chief of the Parisian sports daily newspaper, L'Equipe.

'What has happened is really a good thing for our sport' declared Pariente. 'By the detection of such a big name in such an important event as the Olympic 100 metres an important deterrent has been established.

'Now the process is under way in which it will be surely established what drug-taking Johnson went in for, and who helped him in this, then other leading athletes will be afraid and other coaches will hesitate to tamper with the natural health and strength of their young competitors.'

Pariente was talking about the most serious problem that has ever affected track and field athletics, the sport which was the heart of the

Games revered by the ancient Greeks and which is still the centre-piece of the modern summer Olympics.

Go back more than 170 years, to London's Tottenham Court Road, on 19 August, 1818, and you can see that sporting spite in what was then termed 'pedestrianism' was less subtle, most blatant and sometimes more satisfyingly dealt with by the honest competitor.

In his Sporting Anecdotes (published 1825), Pierce Egan, an outstanding chronicler of old England's rough and ready pastimes, sets the scene of an early controversial 'record' attempt.

'On Wednesday evening, at six o'clock, Blumsell the painter started to go from the corner of Percy Street, Tottenham Court Road, to go beyond the Whetstone Turnpike, a distance of nine miles and a quarter, in one hour. 'On both sides of the way the crowd was immense and the windows of every house filled. It was a truly arduous task and the ease and style with which Blumsell made his way astonished every one present. He had no opportunity for training, as the bet was only made on the preceding Friday.

'Notwithstanding the difficulties he had of being frequently enveloped with gigs, chaises, horsemen and clouds of dust, he shot up Highgate hill with the fleetness of a deer, distancing them all in spite of the exertion of the whip.

'After Blumsell had ascended this steep hill he went two miles over Finchley Common in less than 11 minutes. Unfair means were used to prevent his winning; particularly the interruption of a man who twice crossed him, and whom Blumsell collared and ultimately floored—yet he performed this most extraordinary feat in 1 min. 12 sec. under the time.

'It was, however, brought to a wrangle by the opposite party who insisted he lost it by 2 min. 8 sec. The general opinion is that Blumsell won it and he is the best runner in England.

'It was for the trifling sum of five pounds a side and the painter was to be recompensed for his exertions with a few shillings. His game stood so high in the sporting world that not a bet could be procured against him.'

Sport in Britain in those days, especially pedestrianism and bare fist pugilism, was basically about the working classes competing against each other for small sums of money and the satisfaction of the middle and upper classes wagering upon the result.

One of the exceptions was Captain Robert Barclay Allardyce, a Scottish landowner born in 1779, who hunted, walked and ran (and trained some of the champion boxers) great distances. In 1808 Barclay covered 1,000 miles in 1,000 consecutive hours and earned himself the splendid sum, in that period, of some £16,000.

Money is not necessarily the root of all evil—some sportsmen and women have always been ready to bend the rules simply because winning a gold medal seemed to them the ultimate ego trip.

But studying the history of early 19th century athletics, before the foundation of the Amateur Athletic Association of England and Scotland and the Amateur Athletic Union of America in 1880, we can see the influence that betting had upon fixed races and rioting by crowds.

The often sleazy world has its own terminology. 'Running to the book', 'Roping' and 'Ringing in' which, in turn, could be defined as 'disguising one's running form to keep a generous handicap', 'holding yourself back so as to lose a race' and 'promoters unfairly fixing the handicapping'.

Only a week before the second A.A.A. championships in 1881 there were ugly scenes in a meeting at Birmingham's Aston Lower Grounds. After a local man named Henry Whyatt had been disqualified in the one mile walk, spectators surged across the track shouting: 'Stop the Yankee' as the American E.E. Merrill looked certain to win.

Ironically, in the A.A.A. walk over seven miles a week later, with the police hovering by in case of trouble, the American Merrill threw up his hands and fainted at the half-way mark, leaving the Yorkshireman James Raby to win out on his own.

Reports that Merrill had been overcome by nerves can be understood when it is considered that only the previous week the American had had to leave the Aston ground with a police escort.

The bitter battle in those years to organise properly controlled athletics under an amateur association was led by a pungent critic named Walter Rye, a former athlete and practising solicitor whose comments in the Sporting Gazette sometimes seemed written by a pen dipped in acid.

At a meeting in the Cannon Street Hotel in 1871 to try and clean up the sport, G.P. Rogers of the London Athletic Club had claimed the aim was: 'to put down the attendance of roughs and extirpate betting men and bad language.' This was not strong enough for Rye, there on behalf of the Thames Hare and Hounds club.

Rye proposed: 'it is not desirable to include in this Association clubs who admit as members men who are not gentlemen by position or education.' When someone called for a definition of a gentleman, a Mr A. Saward of South Norwood A.C., said that non-one who kept or was connected with a shop could be included under that heading.

Possibly the most extreme example of sporting spite is quoted in the official centenary history of the Amateur Athletic Association by Peter Lovesey, by the acrimonious Rye on Fred Elborough winner of five Amateur Athletic Club championships at 440 and 880 yards.

Quoth Rye: 'To a certain extent a champion is public property, and I should not be doing my duty if I did not point out that the systematic giving way to habits of inebriation must tell its tale sooner or later, especially on a constitution already undermined by venereal disease.'

What Rye would try to write nowadays on alleged drug-taking in his beloved sport is a thought to make libel specialists rub their hands and lick their lips.

Drug-taking was not unknown, of course, to the pioneers in track and field. Bill Mallon M.D., in a masterly summary of drug-taking in sport, has pointed out that one of the first sports medicine specialists was the ancient physician Galen.

He claimed: 'The rear hooves of an Abyssinian ass, ground up, boiled in oil, and flavoured with rose petals, was the prescription favoured to improve performance.'

Doping, derived from 'dop' a South African drink made up of extract of cola nuts, xanthines and alcohol to improve endurance, was known right through the late 19th century by the most ambitious trainers of cyclists and athletes.

When an athlete from the Soviet Union was found guilty of taking strychnine during the 1991 world athletics championships in Tokyo, it was for sports historians an echo of early Olympic marathon history.

A mixture of sulphate strychnine, egg white and brandy was given to the American runner Thomas Hicks when he was close to collapse at the end of the 1904 Olympic marathon.

Hicks had not broken the rules of the time but he still did not get the winner's ovation. That, and a handshake of congratulations from Alice 'Blue Gown' Roosevelt, daughter of the American President, had already gone, quarter of an hour earlier, to Fred Lorz.

Suffering from cramp, Lorz had dropped out of the race early, around the 5,000 metres mark. A truck driver had given him a lift, the truck had broken down and Lorz, for a joke, decided to continue into the stadium on foot as though he was first man home.

Vilified when his trick was discovered, and threatened with disqualification for life, Lorz the ultimate Olympic jester, became the U.S. marathon champion the following year.

Four years later in London, Italy's Dorando Pietri became a hero by not winning the marathon. Setting a blazing pace and also, it was subsequently claimed, having had help from strychnine-based aids, he paid the price with exhaustion in the stadium. American John Hayes was declared the winner.

When Hayes and Pietri turned professional for a series of 'revenge' races they were merely the first of many to underline the lack of reality in the laws of old fashioned amateurism. As men and women trained harder for success in track and field many of them looked in vain for financial reward or at least enough cash to pay for their training expenses.

Looking back to the Fifties and Sixties, when I first covered international athletics, much bitterness in those days stemmed from the fact that the leading British administrators of the day, Harold Abrahams and Jack Crump, could write and broadcast for cash and keep their honorary status but the athletes had to remain simon pure.

Nowadays a top handful of British athletes can legitimately earn more than £100,000 a year. Even by the end of the Sixties the chief crowd-pullers probably earned, under the counter and only tax-free if they were prepared to take an extra risk, no more than £4,000.

Of course not all athletes from that period wanted professionalism. But even those famous three musketeers from the first four minute mile of May, 1954 Roger Bannister, Chris Chataway and Chris Brasher 'gained' prestige from their athletics prowess for their later careers without actually taking cash to run.

Others in the Seventies, like 10,000 metres record breaker David Bedford and hurdler Alan Pascoe, missed out on the present day official pay-outs which should have rewarded their obvious charisma.

At least Pascoe was able to use his contacts in athletics, and the early experience of promoting at Crystal Palace for Borough Road College, as a springboard to becoming a sports marketing millionaire.

Britain, once the birth place of modern amateurism, deserves credit for setting up in the Eighties a system of subventions—payments on a set scale to athletes for turning out in invitation meetings or even international matches—unthinkable to an older generation who regarded it as an honour to represent their country.

The scale of payment, agreed by the British governing bodies and administered by the powerful chief promotions officer Andy Norman, has led to bitterness and at least one major dispute, never settled satisfactorily, between Norman and former Olympic champion Steve Ovett.

Field events specialists like shot-putter Judy Oakes have argued for long that they have been underpaid for international matches compared with bigger gate attractions like sprinter Linford Christie or miler Peter Elliott.

The official answer is that the payments from a sport whose main revenue is its contract with commercial T.V. plus marketing deals must reflect 'market forces'.

But not all medal winning track athletes are necessarily regarded as equal either.

In the early winter of 1990, only a few months before their successes in the Tokyo world championships, European champions Roger Black (400 metres) and Kriss Akabusi (400 metres hurdles), plus their coach Mike Whittingham, met to thrash out financial racing terms with Norman whom they felt was reluctant to give them their due.

Ironically, it was Black and Akabusi, the following summer, who found themselves 'banned' from the prestigious Weltklasse meeting in Zurich because promoter Andreas Brugger was at logger-heads with their agent John Bicourt.

The dispute was over the commitment to Zurich of Kenyan distance runner Julius Chelimo—also a member of Bicourt's stable just as Elliott's manager and coach, Kim McDonald, handles the competitive programme of a number of other Kenyan stars from his Thamesside office.

Looking back to the old days of the 'brown envelope' or the £5 note in the shoe, the arrival of agents in athletics could obviously be of benefit to the ambitious competitor.

I can recall in Stockholm back in 1982 the Kenyan runner Peter Koech, who had just run 5,000 metres in the excellent time of 13 min. 09. 50, the fourth fastest ever at that date, telling me proudly of his fee. 'Five English pounds' he said . . . .

But even nowadays, when the majority of the Africans coming on to the circuit no longer think in the economic terms of a struggling farmer in their country, a greedy manager could still run some naive Third World competitor ragged round Europe.

One way of controlling such unscrupulous Svengalis is the decision by the International Amateur Athletic Federation to have their world championships every two instead of every four years. This, it is said, will forcibly cut down the number of invitation meetings every two years and put some power back in the hands of the national federations.

Sadly, money will continue to be a source of envy and bitterness in modern track and field especially when so many athletes, including those from Britain, take little heed of the morrow, forgetting that one ruptured hamstring could mean no car, no house, or flat, no real future.

Andy Norman, as a former police officer who has seen at close quarters the problems of the thoughtless young, tried in vain some years ago to interest young athletes in working part time for a major insurance company with the idea that when their athletics was over they would have a full time employer. He had not one favourable response.

He is inclined to agree with my pessimistic prediction that the day will come when young men, up on charges of debt or worse, will claim in the dock that they are broke or accused of theft because 'British athletics let me down.'

Yet there are notable examples of self-help being practised by leading athletes. Tim Hutching, cross-country world championship silver medal winner, kept his mortgage payments going when he was injured by doing television and radio work. Distance runner Eamonn Martin has always combined his vast training with virtually full time work for Fords.

Finally, Fatima Whitbread, so cruelly robbed of at least two whole seasons competition, began coaching work with efficiency and charm and founded the Chafford Hundred club to help market other top British athletes.

As some athletes have made more and more money the voice of the coaches have been heard, wondering aloud as to how much time and effort they could give without expecting some recompense from their charges.

A notable dispute in this area was that between Liz McColgan, later to become world 10,000 metres champion, and her erstwhile coach John Anderson, previously mentor of world 5,000 metres record breaker David

Moorcroft. Anderson, once McColgan took on a manager in Kim McDonald and said that her husband Peter would coach her in future, decided to seek redress in the courts.

McColgan, whose peak annual earnings before Tokyo, she had told me, were about £97,000, seemed likely to attract income of at least double that following her gold medal in Japan.

An alternative view of how the coaches should survive was given in September 1991 by coach Frank Horwill in the magazine Athletics Weekly.

Wrote Horwill: 'The first coach that I know of to charge a fee was Franz Stampfl who requested the sum of 10 pence to take part in his sessions at Parliament Hill from 1955 to 1959. He always had a big attendance.

'Current discussion on the subject is based on the assumption that it is the athlete who must pay the coach. I think this is wrong. The United Kingdom Coaching Committee should pay coaches and not the athlete . . . If they are good enough to produce internationals for the British team they are good enough to be paid for their time and effort.'

Horwill suggested a sliding scale of from £50 for coaching a senior county winner up to a ceiling of £800 for producing a world or Olympic champion. This is, of course, almost incredibly modest when one considers that Carl Lewis's 100 metres victory in world record time in Tokyo in 1991 was reckoned to be worth anywhere between £1,500,000 and £4,000,000 to that greatest of all athletes.

The coach-athlete situation remains muddled with many different interpretations and attitudes. Ron Roddan, who has done so much for Linford Christie over the years, is a retired bachelor who suggests money from athletics is not that important to him, adding: 'Linford looks after me.'

Mike Whittingham, who coaches both Kriss Akabusi and Roger Black, is a young married man with a full time job in leisure. He still would not have made the costly trip to Tokyo but for having his fare paid by athletics benefactor Eddie Kulukundis who, the same summer, covered the travel costs of several other coaches to the European junior championships in Thessalonika.

Whittingham, it could be argued, should have had his Tokyo costs paid by the British Board. Alternatively, he was perhaps a little diffident in not already having made an agreement to take at least a share of his expense from the competitive earning fees of his champions.

We can trace a great deal of the decline in behaviour in athletics to the arrival of 'wads of money' and to the fact that the sport which still laughably calls itself 'amateur' cannot come to terms with the existence of filthy lucre.

The athletes themselves often seem to want all the independence of being, ostensibly, an amateur, without taking on the true pro's responsibility.

Time and again, right back to the days of Seb Coe and Steve Ovett, the first real money earners of the track in Britain, competitors have insisted that they do not take on races for financial reasons but only 'because it fits in with the season's plans of me and my coach.'

I believe that many of these protestations are phony, bringing an extra shroud of artificiality to a Grand Prix and European invitational circuit which can sometimes look very plastic with its record attacks and carefully separated A and B sprint event fields.

However, the introduction of the Mobil Grand Prix was, on the whole, a 'good thing' as the authors of 1066 And All That would have said. The I.A.A.F. could see that unless they put up a summer schedule involving some attractive cash prizes they were going to lose most of their power in the United States with the boom of marathon and other road racing.

The complicated points system which produces overall Grand Prix champions at the end of every season has never caught on with the European media. But the tussle amongst European promoters and sports oriented European companies to be associated with the Grand Prix has benefited the sport.

Danger signs appeared, however, during the continental recessional summers of 1990 and 1991 when the sporting programme of much of the former Eastern block crumbled and some Western meetings had to withdraw from the calendar through lack of sponsorship.

This will and may still continue to be a challenge to the greed of certain leading athletes and their agents.

Holland's former long distance world record breaker Jos Hermans has been busily pushing Germany's glamorous sprint queen Katrin Krabbe towards an income of more than a million dollars since her double gold medal in Tokyo.

But as a promoter of the annual Hengelo meeting Hermans complains:

'Everyone wants to run nowadays and everyone wants more money. The world's athletes are in for a shock—they are in danger of drinking the well dry and their attitude will drive away many potential sponsors on whom we depend.'

Wilfred Meert, a Belgian newspaperman who runs the annual Memorial van Damme meeting in Brussels, says: 'Athletes don't realise that many sponsors only want to know if you have one or two special athletes competing, Carl Lewis for example. Tell the sponsor about most other athletes, however good, and they just shrug. It's a tough, real world out there, you see.'

Considering the amount of pressure, the amount of mortgages at stake nowadays, behaviour during competition has not declined noticeably.

Perhaps that made the headlines all the bigger when, at the 1990 A.A.A. championships, the crowd at Birmingham came close to seeing a punch-up during the final of the men's 1,500 metres. Even the specialist magazine Athletics Today headlined its cover page High Drama at Birmingham . .

Tempers Rise in the Heat.

What happened was that the 1,500 metres field, racing for the chance to represent Britain in the European championships in Split, had reached the last backstraight when steeplechaser Mark Rowland suddenly moved up to the outside of the pack.

Simon Halliday responded by trying to move through a gap which was really too small and in the resulting confusion he forced Tony Morrell and himself off the track and totally out of the race.

It was then that the crowd, the press box and a vast television audience saw an outraged Morrell raise his hand at Halliday. At the time some observers, though not those of us who also report boxing, believed Morrell had connected with a punch. But even Halliday confirmed that the 27 year old from Hartlepool had missed.

Subsequently Rowland was rather doubtfully disqualified and appealed, Neil Horsfield became the most instantly forgotten A.A.A. champion and Morrell was given a formal warning for bringing the sport into disrepute. Halliday, who had been involved physically with Morell the previous year, escaped censure.

Athletics Today called for a more severe sentence on Morrell, saying that he should have been told he was no longer in consideration for Split. For me this was an over reaction. Some runners are clumsier than others, especially Morrell who was to fall in the Zurich meeting that summer and again in Oslo the next year.

No wonder promoter Andy Norman dryly told him: 'In future I'll be paying you by the lap—it's safer.'

The main reason for rough and tumble in the middle distance—Peter Elliott of Britain falling in the 1,500 metres heats in Split, Steve Cram baulked in the Tokyo first round—is the over frequent use of pace-makers at 800 and 1,500 metres.

When it comes to championship races the inexperienced runners all bunch up together, looking in vain for a rabbit to take up the pace, and elbows and ankles are bound to mingle dangerously.

In both Split and Tokyo the decision of the British manager Les Jones to protest on behalf of his athletes was regarded by the athletes and officials of other countries as doubtful sporting behaviour—almost sharp practice.

As it happened, Elliott later expressed some doubts about action taken on his behalf, having been subjected to booing while he was warming-up for the final. In Tokyo the Spanish Federation filed a counter-protest, suggesting wryly that Britain were making too much of a habit of this and getting over-fair treatment, too.

Perhaps. But remembering past lack of militancy by British team officials I think that Jones, a Belfast Customs officer who must be professionally accustomed to human duplicity, was probably right to have a go on both occasions.

Certainly Britain was right, and backed by many other European countries, to protest at the end of the 1991 European Cup in Frankfurt when a 4 × 400 metres Russian relay runner clearly ran outside his lane.

I would also have liked to have seen another protest on that day, following the last leg of the women's 4 × 400 metres relay when Germany's Grit Breuer bumped Britain's Linda Keough briefly off the track at the end of the backstraight.

Lack of official diligence rather than officiousness over-shadowed the unforgettable 100 metres men's final in the Tokyo world championships. Even the official results book shows that the American Dennis Mitchell, winner of the bronze medal ahead of Britain's Linford Christie, got away with a flying start.

There, beside Mitchell's name, is an asterisk next to his reaction time, off the blocks, of 0.090 sec. Then, most pointedly, comes this extract from the I.A.A.F. rules:

'The starter shall be the sole judge of any fact connected with the start of the race. . . . the starting blocks must be linked to a false start apparatus for the assistance of the starters.

'The apparatus shall emit an acoustic signal, audible to the starter, whenever the reaction detected by the apparatus is less than 100/1000ths of a second. If the starter decides that there has been a false start, he may consult the reaction times on the false start apparatus in order to confirm which athlete(s) is/are responsible for the false start.'

All those words add up to this simple fact. The Japanese starter for the 100 metres final, just like his colleagues in some other races, declined to wear the acoustic ear-phones which would have allowed him instantly to detect that Mitchell had 'broken' and to command a recall.

Now the I.A.A.F. are seriously considering that the ear-phones, instead of just being an offer as an aid, must become compulsory for the starter in events where the results can be decided by 1/100th of a second.

The history of innovation in modern athletics has seen the experiment and then banning of a built-up shoe for high jumping and a brush spike shoe for sprinting. As well as a swiftly banned 'Spanish javelin throwing' method whereby the athlete soaped his hand and then spun in a circle before dangerously hurling the spear in almost any direction.

But nothing was more blatant than the story of the long jump in the world championships of Rome in 1987. The 'fixing' of the bronze medal for Italy's Giovanni Evangelista rather than the American Larry Myricks was proved by an Italian T.V. channel which came up with computer analysis of videotapes of the event.

These indicated that Evangelista's sixth and last jump had been lengthened by at least half a metre and recorded as a fake 8 metres 38. Up to then Evangelista had been in fourth position with 8 metres 19 and Myricks was third with 8 metres 33.

23

This appalling example of misconduct, which reflected so seriously on the Italian hosts, was at first seemingly ignored by the I.A.A.F., which had and still has an Italian president. They confirmed the 'official' results even though the unfortunate Evangelista, who had never asked for such distasteful favouritism, publicly stated that he wanted to return his medal.

Eventually the Italian Olympic Committee opened its own investigation which finally clarified the misbehaviour of the judges at the long jump and commented on negligence on the part of higher officials in dealing with the case.

If this seems the most Machiavellian story from one of athletics' seemingly most straightforward events it is worth considering a story from the West German championships of 1960 which was only revealed, 31 years later, in the I.A.A.F.'s progression of world best performances by Ekkehard zur Megede and Richard Hymans.

On his fourth jump that day the German athlete Manfred Steinbach had his leap measured at 8 metres 14. That was just one centimetre further than the world record by the immortal American all-rounder Jesse Owens which had stood since 25 May 1935. Sadly for Steinbach, the following wind was then announced as 3.2 metres per second compared with the allowable limit of 2 metres.

Only now do we know that the official in charge of the long jump, Walter Blume later admitted that by error there had been no wind gauge reading taken for that particular jump.

Blume said privately: 'We would have been blamed by the public if we had confessed our mistake. So I decided to give a fictitious reading, of course more than the permitted 2.0, so that it was not necessary to fill in a record protocol.' Then Blume added: 'You may publish this after my death.' A most poignant postscript in view of the fact that the wind measured for all of Steinbach's other jumps that day never exceeded 1.1 metres.

Still, right now, as we approach the end of the 20th century track and field athletics' most serious problem remains that of drug-taking. It is possible that the deterrents are working, that the mild optimism of the I.A.A.F.'s Dr Arne Ljundqvist, with whom I talked in Tokyo in 1991, is justified.

Ljundqvist had hoped for no 'positive' doping tests in Tokyo. In the event he still got only two and believes that education about drugs is working right across the world including the United States where, rather than in Eastern Europe, the whole nasty business began in horse racing.

Still, what can we think when we consider the tale of one of Britain's young athletes attending the 1991 European junior championships in Thessalonika.

Discus thrower Glen Smith, aged only 19, the U.K. record holder, claims he was approached by a Soviet competitor when he was competing in a junior international in Espoo, Finland.

'He asked me back to his hotel room' said Smith 'and claimed that the anabolic steroids he wanted to sell me would put five metres on my throw and 20 kilos on any weight lifts.

'He showed me packets containing 300 tablets which he said would last 40 weeks. He told me that 12 days before competing you stop taking them so you don't have any problems with drug tests. He has a personal doctor and he is also told when he is going to be drug tested.'

Smith, who reported the approach officially to the British junior team's chief coach, summed up: 'I wanted to know whether I was competing against steroid users. Afterwards I felt like hitting him. I felt as if I'd been kicked in the teeth.'

Only if hundreds of thousands of other young competitors share Glen Smith's sense of outraged fair play will international athletics truly be clean.

BOXING

Neil Allen

Turn back the pages of the long and colourful history of the ring and there, in the 19th century prime of bare-fist pugilism, the great English essayist William Hazlitt provides proof that boxing's bad boys are nothing new.

'Our friend (Tom Hickman) had vapoured and swaggered too much', wrote Hazlitt' as if he wanted to grin and bully his adversary out of the fight.

'This is the grave-digger, would Tom Hickman exclaim in the moments of intoxication from gin and successes, showing his tremendous right hand.

'Why should he threaten to inflict dishonourable chastisement on my old master Richmond, a veteran going off the stage? Magnaminity, my dear Tom, and bravery, should be inseparable . . . .

'Or why should he go up to his antagonist, the first time he ever saw him at the Fives Court, and measuring him from head to foot, as Achilles surveyed Hector, say to him:

'What, are you Bill Neate? I'll knock more blood out of that great carcase (sic) of thine, this day fortnight, than you ever knock'd out of a bullock's!'

'It was not manly, 'twas not fighter-like. If he was sure of the victory (as he was not), the less said the better. The best men were always the best behaved.

'A boxer was bound to beat his man, but not to thrust his fist, either actually or by implication, in every one's face. Even a highwayman, in the way of trade, may blow out your brains, but if he uses foul language at the same time, I would say he is no gentleman.'

No-one ever more clearly summed up the moral code of sporting behaviour than Hazlitt in this preamble to the bare-fist championship fight of 1821 in which Bill Neate soundly thrashed the over-confident Gas Man, Thomas Hickman.

Almost 170 years later, on the third weekend in February, 1991, in towns as far apart in miles and culture as Brighton, England and Las Vegas, U.S.A. boxing's capacity to provide controversy was again at its most provocative.

At the Sussex seaside resort made famous by Royal patronage in the Regency period, an aloof, smooth-faced young man named Chris Eubank was defending one of the four versions of the world middleweight title against Canadian challenger Dan Sherry.

Meanwhile, in Vegas, the gambling capital of the western world, Hector Camacho from Puerto Rico was tangling with American Greg Haugen, then the owner of the light-welterweight title belt of the World Boxing Organisation.

In England that night the 24 year old Eubank had opened proceedings with a typical piece of bravado, vaulting the ropes into the ring as the music of his theme tune, 'Simply the Best', was being played.

Before the opening bell Sherry marched across the canvas, seeking an eyeball to eyeball confrontation, only for Eubank, blank-eyed, to walk right round him, leaving the Canadian sheepishly facing up to a ring post.

Early in the opening round, Sherry found himself briefly on the floor from a left jab. More significant of the tasteless, teasing way the match would go was a 10 sec, dramatic, mid-ring pose by Eubank after the round had ended before he chose to return to his corner.

In the third round Sherry was warned by referee Frank Santore for hitting on the back of the neck. At the end of the fifth he actually spat at the champion and from then on the harassment increased, with Sherry, surely ahead on points in a bout starved of real action, shouting and sneering and exaggeratedly imitating Eubank's laid back style.

Near the end of the ninth Eubank caught Sherry with a smashing right hand uppercut which lacerated the Canadian's lower lip.

Victory in his sights, Eubank attacked in the 10th. When Eubank at last caught up the two half fell into the ropes. There Eubank, finding himself facing the wrong way, with his back to Sherry, brought a gasp from ringsiders as he jerked back his head with a butt which landed on Sherry's forehead.

Referee Santore, jumping in to warn Eubank for his palpable infringement, gave Sherry a shove backwards. The Canadian knelt down, then sank to the floor, rising and falling several times in apparent distress.

'He's faking . . . he's bottled it' came the cries from the pro-Eubank crowd though subsequent medical evidence suggested that Sherry was concussed and also in trouble because of blood he had inhaled from his cut lip.

With Sherry unable to continue, referee Santore called for the scoring cards of three World Boxing Organisation judges, Frank Cairo, Torben Hansen and John Rupert, after having instructed all the officials to deduct two points from Eubank's score for that apparently deliberate backward butt.

Then came the announcement of the scores. At 95 to 93 points Cairo voted for Sherry. Then Hansen went the other way for Eubank and Rupert allowed him to keep the world title with a 95—92 score.

While the still collapsed Sherry was taken away by stretcher, a section of the crowd booed the technical decision in favour of Eubank and the champion suggested, purely on his say so, that he had become upset when Sherry called him 'a nigger'.

That charge was subsequently denied by Sherry whose trainer and whose backer, Sugar Ray Leonard, were both black.

It was left to the British Boxing Board of Control to fine winner and still champion Eubank £10,000 for having brought the sport into disrepute.

If this had been a ringside evening out to remember, how about Haugen against Camacho in Las Vegas the same weekend?

Tempers had risen, at least in the crowd, even before the opening bell.

Hector 'Macho Man' Camacho had made a crass attempt to cash in on the Gulf War which had opened only minutes before the fighters entered the ring. The Puerto Rican was dressed not in a normal boxing robe but camouflage uniform and helmet, with the addition of a general's insignia of four stars.

Bad taste was followed eventually by bad feeling at the opening of the 12th and final round of a close fight when referee Carlos Padilla brought the two fighters together for the traditional hand-shake, the touching of gloves, for the last three minutes of action.

Haugen, a seven to one underdog, refused to touch gloves even after Padilla had again tried to bring the men together. Camacho extended his right glove. Still Haugen, who was to admit the following day that he had been deliberately baiting Camacho, declined.

Then Camacho blew his top, firing three punches over the referee's shoulder, all of them missing. The irate Padilla promptly took a point away from Camacho, a point which was to prove vital when the judges' decisions were announced just a few minutes later.

Padilla said later: 'I asked them three times, in the name of sportsmanship, to touch gloves. I know they don't like each other but when Camacho jumped in he committed a foul. He deliberately and intentionally did it. It's not a question of whether he hit Haugen or not.'

Dalby Shirely was to give his verdict to Camacho, 114—112 but Bill McConkie (114—112) and Art Lure (114—113) combined to give Haugen the nod and Camacho his first defeat in 12 years and 39 fights.

The point deduction for those three missed punches had cost Camacho not only his W.B.O. light-welterweight title but also a $5 million pay-day against Julio Cesar Chavez.

But had it?

The aftermatch was to prove even more bizarre. A post-fight drug test by the Nevada State Athletic Commission was found, four days after the fight, to be positive, for marijuana in the case of Haugen.

Haugen, who admitted to the Nevada Commission that he had smoked marijuana 'on and off for 15 years' was fined $25,000, told to contribute 200 hours of community service and accept drug counselling. Finally, he had to accept a return bout with Camacho three months later.

On May 18 in Las Vegas, Camacho again had a point taken away from him by the referee Bobby Ferrera—this time for hitting Haugen after the bell to end the 11th when Haugen had wound him up by standing nose to nose and glaring.

Camacho was so sure he had lost that, temperament getting the better of him once again, he stalked out of the ring without waiting to hear the verdict.

But when the judges' cards were called for it was Bert Clemens (115—112) for Haugan but both Doug Tucker (115-112) and Dave Moretti (114-113) handing back the W.B.O. title to the Macho Man.

Mind you, the behaviour of the Puerto Rican had been almost compassionate compared with what took place at Hornchurch, Essex on April 15, 1795.

It was there that Daniel Mendoza, the fighting pride of Aldgate, lost the championship of England to one Gentleman John Jackson who belied his nickname, but not the rules of the time, by seizing Mendoza's long hair with one hand and then pummelling him into defeat with the other.

The first rules of the Noble Art of Self Defence, or the Ignoble Art as the late Dr Edith Summerskill, a boxing abolitionist, labelled it, were drawn up by a champion, Jack Broughton from Cirencester in 1743.

Broughton also invented gloves, known as 'mufflers' to save the wealthy gentlemen who came to spar with him 'from the inconveniency of black eyes, broken jaws and bloody noses.' Broughton was well aware of the dangers of the ring—his challenger George Stevenson died after their fight.

The highlights of those first rules, as important attempt to bring discipline to the brutal old game, were as follows:

'A square of one yards drawn in the centre of the stage, to which boxers are brought to face one another at the start and after each fall.

A man has 30 seconds after a fall to return to the square otherwise he is beaten.

Each boxer to choose an umpire to settle disputes. If they cannot agree, a third is picked and his word final.

No person is to hit his Adversary when he is down, or seize him by the ham, the breeches, or any part below the waist: a man on his knees to be reckoned down.'

These rules 'as agreed by several Gentlemen at Broughton's Ampitheatre, Tottenham Court Road, August 16, 1743' were to be unaltered, though not always strictly observed, for nearly 100 years, until the New London Prize Ring Rules of 1838.

Amongst the most important clarifications of the new rules was that the ring, for fights staged on turf or wooden boards, should be 'four and twenty feet square'.

An outer ring was occupied by the two umpires and the referee and the backers of the two fighters and protected, as much as was possible, from the fight mob by prizefighters armed with sticks or horsewhips.

Rules 13 to 17 listed in 1838 made fouls of kicking, butting, gouging, biting and falling on a man with the knees. Fighters now had to come up to a single line called the 'scratch' and they had to do so unassisted by their seconds.

The last major bareknuckle championship under the London rules was on July 8 1889 at Richburg, Mississippi where John L. Sullivan, the Boston Strong Boy, licked Jake Kilrain after 75 rounds or 2 hours 16 minutes.

During the 45th round of the brawl, staged in blazing heat, Sullivan who had been sick five rounds earlier, knocked Kilrain down and then jumped on his stomach. Not until the 75th round, just after Kilrain's corner had been ready to be paid to surrender, did the referee award the match to Sullivan.

Some years later, when the Queensberry rules (strictly timed three minute rounds, a minute's rest between rounds, the use of gloves) were introduced and enforced by the National Sporting Club in London, ruthless old John L. welcomed them:' The prize ring rules allow too much leeway for the rowdy element' he declared.

'Such mean tricks as spiking, biting, falling down without being struck, scratching with the nails, strangling . . . are impossible under the Queensberry Rules. Fighting under them before gentlemen is a pleasure.'

With the introduction of the million dollar gate era of the 1920s and the two heavyweight world title fights between Jack Dempsey and Gene Tunney, boxing gained much needed respectability.

But just because Dempsey married a film star, Tunney an heiress and British flyweight Jimmy Wilde boxed before the Prince of Wales did not mean the end of bad behaviour in or out of the ring.

Fritzie Zivic, a world welterweight champion from Pittsburgh who had 230 professional fights between 1931 and 1949, explained it succinctly long after he retired.

'I was given a label as a dirty fighter but I never lost a fight on a foul in my life. I'd give them the head, choke them, hit 'em in the balls.

'But never in my life I used my thumb because I wanted no-one to use it on me. Sure, I used to bang 'em pretty good. You're fighting, you're not playing the piano, you know.'

Billy Conn, an Irish American light-heavyweight who came excitingly close to beating the great Joe Louis from the world heavyweight title, was known as a classic boxing stylist.

But looking back with interviewer Peter Heller, Conn provided two especially salty memories of his time in the ring, the first from a fight with Freddie Apostoli.

'I remember I got in an argument with him. We stepped back and called each other all the names. I said 'Listen you dago bastard, keep your thumb out of my eye!' He says: 'Listen, you Irish son of a bitch, quite beefin' and c'mon and fight.'

'We were hot at one another. They put the microphone under the ring because they could hear us swearing for 19 rows back. It was being short-waved right round the world . . . .'

Then there was a fight with heavyweight Bob Pastor recalled Conn.

'Bob was a nice fellow. I didn't like his manager. I hit Pastor in the balls so he started beefing. I hit him low again and I said 'Now I'm really going to hit you in the balls, you big crybaby.'

'I hit him in the balls and knocked his ass through the ropes in the 13th round. You're supposed to do anything you can to win, see? You're not an altar boy in there. Hit 'em on the break, backhand, do all the rotten stuff to 'em. Are they going to shoot you for it?'

Old fighters like Zivic and Conn may choose to exaggerate the violence of their youth. Certainly the majority of the thousands of amateur and professional fights I have watched have been boxed within the letter of the rules if not always the spirit.

But the really polished, accomplished pro can be so proficient in the dirty tricks department that neither referee nor ringside reporter can easily catch him out.

Zivic was once supposed to have said admiringly of five times world middleweight champion Sugar Ray Robinson: 'He was so clever and so dirty he could make you bust your own eye open'—Ray's secret being that he could pull the opponent forward in such a way that the victim's brows collided with the boniest part of the Robinson skull.

Britain's talented world light-heavyweight champion in the Seventies, John Conteh, also had the reputation, amongst the seconds of some of those who fought him, of being able to pull a stroke or two inside the ropes. Yet John, with that charming, disarming smile of his, can point out that he never lost a single pro fight on a disqualification.

The control exercised by British referees in the ring continues to be pretty complete even if noone would agree with all the points decisions they render. On a rare occasion when a referee was endangered by a fighter's actions at a Wembley promotion the boxer was promptly banned by the British Boxing Board of Control.

Where the Board does, in my opinion, lack sufficient control is in checking the drastic weight-reducing undergone by many of our professionals when training for a match.

After losing the International Boxing Federation's cruiserweight world title, Britain's Glenn McCrory said that at one stage he was shedding poundage so painfully to make the 13 st. 8 lb. limit that his face 'looked like an Auchswitz victim.' Former world flyweight title holder Duke McKenzie, who later won a second international belt as a bantamweight, has also told of the agonies of dieting he endured to make the flyweight limit of 8 st.

McKenzie claimed that no one in his camp know what he was doing. But in many other cases managers and trainers are taking fearful risks with the health of their boxers. An even partially dehydrated, half starved man could be risking his life when he climbs through the ropes.

What makes the modern weight-reducing so tragic is that extra divisions, like light-welterweight (10st.) and light-middleweight (11st.) have been deliberately introduced into the sport, both nationally and internationally, so that boxers have more championships for which to aim.

Risks taken by corner-men with cut-sealing lotions is watched for with hawk-like attention by the Board's inspectors. They know that though a cut may be staunched with apparent success, anyone using a substance outside the Board's regulations could risk blinding the boxer when the 'concrete' is dug out later in the dressing-room.

In at least a couple of major matches I believe, from my own observation at ringside, that the Board's men missed out in catching guilty 'cuts men'. But on the whole the deterrent works with massive success, aided by the responsibility towards their boxer of most trainers.

We have certainly advanced a little from the time when Dave Charnley, an outstanding British lightweight of the Fifties, came back to his corner with a cut eye only to find that his elderly second began treating the uninjured optic.

'Hey, it's the other eye that's gone', protested Charnley. But all in vain. 'Don't be fussy' replied the old retainer, labouring on.

Crowd behaviour, as in several other sports, continues to remain a problem in British boxing for the Board and the promoters who sometimes find that hyping-up a match, with fighters slanging each other off in the build-up, can back-fire on the night.

Those of us who were there will not forget the drunken, violent behaviour of some 'fans' on the late, long night when American heavyweight Tim Witherspoon beat Frank Bruno in 1986 and the rain of cans which descended upon the heads of 'Marvellous' Marvin Hagler and his retinue within moments of his world middleweight victory in 1980 over Alan Minter.

Those two disgraceful incidents, the first certainly fuelled by alcohol, the second possibly by racists, gave Britain a bad reputation in the United States where the few examples of unruly public behaviour at fights have mostly come from events featuring and attended by volatile Latin-Americans.

Without a ban on the sale of alcohol in the arena and sufficient stewarding and policing (a costly item) there is still no guarantee that a major British promotion will be free from trouble outside the ring.

At the first Chris Eubank-Michael Watson middleweight fight in 1991 at Olympia there was a classic example of how intelligent stewarding can avoid confrontation. During the preliminary bouts a black spectator insisted on standing by the fenced off press and guest area a few feet from the ring. It was obvious that his illegal presence there would soon encourage others to move forward from their seats, forming a potential trouble area.

After a white steward had several times politely asked the man to move back without success, a subsequent, similar request from a black steward met with acceptance. Less than an hour later the hall was in a vocal uproar at the most unpopular decision in favour of Eubank but there was enough room in the immediate ring area for the loudly booed winner to be escorted from his corner to his dressing-room.

On another occasion, in the cheerful cockpit atmosphere of north London's York Hall, a roughhouse postscript to the defeat of West Ham's Mark Kaylor by James Cook in a European super-middleweight (12 st.) title fight was only averted by Kaylor's manager Jimmy Tibbs. As one group of supporters moved menacingly towards the opposition, Tibbs jumped between them, shouting until he was listened to and obeyed.

American colleagues take understandable pleasure in citing cases of British crowd behaviour, including Tony Sibson's 1988 middleweight fight with Frank Tate in Stafford when some form of tear gas pellets were let off in the arena.

The scenes from Stafford, with outraged remarks from an American commentator, were shown live to a vast media audience gathered in Calgary for the Winter Olympics of that year and gave many American managers the excuse to ask for 'danger money' the next time they were asked to bring their fighters to Britain.

But American boxing provided its own show of ugliness in the ring of The Mirage casino, Las Vegas at the end of the first Mike Tyson-Razor Ruddock heavyweight fight in March 1991.

Referee Richard Steele set off the row by halting the fight in 2min. 22sec. of the seventh round when Ruddock had reeled backward onto the ropes. Many there felt that Ruddock, who regained his feet and indicated he could continue, should have been allowed to do so.

That was not my opinion. I felt rather that Steele, who was to leave the ring under heavy guard, deserved to be criticised for the number fouls he allowed Tyson to commit during the fight.

All that mattered to more interested parties was to seek some kind of basic justice in the ring against the other camp. For several minutes, while both Tyson and Ruddock managed to stay aloof from these extra-mural matters, the ring was full of heaving, scuffling figures.

Murad Muhammad, Ruddock's promoter, appeared to be in the thick of the action aiming kicks at the head of Tyson's trainer, Richie Giachetti who had been wrestled to the floor.

Later Muhammad was to say: 'I wouldn't put me on any kind of kicking team, 'cause I'd miss.'

When the State of Nevada Athletic Commission opened its enquiry into the fracas, seven weeks after the fight, Muhammad did not appear, retaining instead the services of a Vegas lawyer.

It is possible of course to take the Nevada Commission less than seriously. Writer Jonathan Bailey describes it as consisting of 'a veterinarian, an insurance agent, a Reno hotelier, the owner of four MacDonald franchises and a doctor who prescribed diet pills to Elvis Presley.'

However that may be, the Commission's prosecutor took seriously enough what Murad Muhammad had appeared to be trying to do inside the ring.

'I've prosecuted homicides before when there was no weapon involved and in almost every instance the death is occasioned by a boot to the head . . . The fact that Mr Giachetti got a split lip or an abrasion speaks only of the bad aim of Mr Muhammad.'

The argument that Muhammad was trying to defend Delroy Ruddock, Razor's brother, from a choke hold or strangle hold by Giachetti, and resorted to kicking because he was too fat to bend down, did not impress the commission.

They suspended Muhammad's promoter's license for a year and levied a fine of $25,000. After an appeal by Muhammad that his actions had been caused by sleep deprivation the decision was upheld . . . only for a re-trial to be granted.

In an interim judgement, Boxing Illustrated commented: 'The only certainty is that the sport of boxing once again humiliated itself.'

As the world heavyweight championship goes, so goes boxing. The adage certainly rings true from the days when Jack Dempsey and Joe Louis lent dignity to the crown and Rocky Marciano walked and talked and fought like every American boy's comic book hero.

Iron Mike Tyson, who first became undisputed champion in August 1987, is one of the most exciting fighters I have ever seen and in close range interviews has been a pleasure to work with, possessing an extraordinary knowledge of boxing history for one so young.

But you are bound to wonder about his influence ever since his first unforgettable quote following his 1986 fight with Jesse Ferguson.

'I always try' said young Mike 'to catch them right on the tip of the nose because I try to push the bone into the brain.'

He was joking then, Tyson told us later; he didn't know any better as a young kid from the rough side of New York. But the vicious street talk, the brief spurts of rage, the allegations of sexual indiscretions have continued, possibly increased since Tyson suffered his first loss of James 'Buster' Douglas and did himself no favours by not accepting defeat gracefully.

It is, of course, too much to expect Tyson, a product of reform school whom boxing and trainer Cus D'Amato probably saved from a life in prison or early death, to come over like Sir Galahad.

'I guess I'm a bit of a psychopath' he once lisped cheerily to us during a long talk in Atlantic City. 'What will they say about me when I'm dead?' he asked me another time. 'That I lived like a dog?'

'With all he's been through, it's remarkable he's still around' says veteran corner man Angelo Dundee.

'I feel sorry for the kid. The outbursts, the ugliness are a result of frustration. It's unforgivable to be that way.

'Loose is better. You gotta have fun. You gotta be loose as a goose. You got a license to be loose when you're talented.'

Angelo Dundee was, of course, the trainer of the loosest of them all, Muhammad Ali. A champion whose behaviour was often outrageous but never vicious, a man whose sense of fun made him the most loved of all those strange creatures—professional fighters.

Sad that we don't quite feel like smiling when we're around him any more these days.

CRICKET

John Thicknesse

It is a moot point whether it reflects more credit on the modern cricketer, or more shame on D.R. Jardine, that despite a world that becomes audibly nastier and unmistakably more vicious every year, the occurrence that brought the game its greatest notoriety, and wrecked more friendships, happened 60 years ago.

Judged purely in terms of the danger in which it placed batsmen, Bodyline, having been truly menacing in the hands only of its main practitioner, Harold Larwood, almost certainly posed less of a physical threat than the high-speed, four-pronged, pace attacks fielded by the West Indies since 1976, and possibly also than by Dennis Lillee and Jeff Thomson as they bowled together in successive series against England and the West Indies in Australia in the middle 1970s.

But Bodyline caused a deeper rift, and longer-lasting bitterness, between Test teams than any event before or since—including even sledging, the most repellent development of the modern game—and for a simple reason. It was an anachronism. It hit cricket when the game was played with what contemporary players would regard as quite absurd decorum. Suddenly, out of the blue, appeared a captain, Jardine, who hated his Australian opposition with such intensity he was seemingly prepared to go to any lengths to beat them, and who had at his command the fastest and most accurate fast bowler of his time, the 5ft 8in Larwood. Jardine was ruthless and relentless, Larwood brilliant, the pitches mostly quick and of uneven bounce, Don Bradman neutralised. He averaged a mere 56.57 compared to 139.14, aged 21, two years before in England; and Jardine, reviled, took the Ashes home 4-1. Someone who had taught him when he was a Winchester schoolboy said before the tour that England 'might win a rubber and lose a Dominion' and he was not far from being right.

Because of a change of law regarding legside field settings, Bodyline as Larwood bowled it could not be bowled today. But in every other respect—intent to intimidate through the pace and especially the length of much fast bowling—spectators see it every time the West Indies take the field. (The same would go for every country if they had fast bowlers of sufficient speed and quality). And by and large no one turns a hair. We are inured to it. Take away the freak of Bodyline—three months in 1932/33—and just about the only similarity between today's game and the one of, not 60 or 50 years ago but as relatively recently as the 1960s, is that the pitch is 22 yards long.

Many terrible things have happened in cricket in the meantime, all reflecting a decline in the ethics of the game. But much as I regret them, I believe the real world—life outside the boundary—has changed faster for the worse. Among the many cricketers I canvassed assembling this survey, former Australian captain Richie Benaud, and John Inverarity, who led Western Australia to four Sheffield Shield titles in the 1970s, both subscribed to the theme that cricket is a mirror of society, a view proposed first in the 19th Century. I would go further. Despite all its unpleasant developments, I think cricket has changed for the worse markedly less than society at large. Never mind famine, disease and drugs, the global calamities. Open your eyes in High Street shops and your ears in public places, and reflect on the baseness that almost unnoticed has become a daily feature of our lives.

There is nothing the matter with cricket that is not instantly curable by goodwill between captains. And if the captains cannot hit it off, by strong umpires. And if neither of those conditions hold, by Boards of Control determined to preserve the best traditions of the game, which for me are sportsmanship and humour. In the last 10 or 20 years, especially since Kerry Packer's World Series Cricket breakaway in Australia in 1977, we have seen all too little of all three.

But Graham Gooch and Vivien Richards showed it could be done in the England-West Indies Test series of 1991. In Gooch, thankfully, England had a captain who had no time for sledging—which is not to say he might not turn a deaf ear to it when used by teammates in self-defence—and in Richards one who was determined to leave the game respected not only as a batsman but as a man of stature. In the latter respect he had some catching up to do, having on England's tours of the West Indies in 1985/86 and 1989/90 twice been at the centre of disgraceful on-field scenes. But in England in 1991 he was exemplary, and the upshot was a series that proved that Test cricket could still be a game rather than a battle.

But—just in case—the International Cricket Council brought in a Code of Conduct*, and instituted independent referees. More than likely both were necessary, and would work—always provided ICC had the courage to exercise their powers when teams or players overstepped the mark. The sadness was that had England's 1991 series with West Indies happened 10 years sooner, and its recipe been followed throughout the 1980s, ICC's measures might never have been needed. But that is wishful thinking, as I am very well aware.

Why? Because many, if not most, of the ills of modern Test cricket stem

* See Addenda page 49.

from inadequate umpiring, which in the eyes of the touring team almost invariably means biassed umpiring. Superficially, it is strange that in a game where players from a diversity of backgrounds—national, social, ethnic and religious—almost always play contentedly in the same county teams as one another, they become suspicious and mistrustful in opposition in their country's Test XIs. But it is only sad, not strange. Any doubt there might have been of the existence of raging xenophobia in cricket disappeared when Richards strongly implied he believed the ICC's experimental restriction on bouncers stemmed from racial jealousy.

'No-one complained when Lillee and Thomson were firing them in short at us in the 1975/6 series in Australia when we were humiliated 5-1,' he wrote in 1991 in his ghosted column in a national newspaper (The Daily Telegraph). 'People said then that we were wimps and cowards and had no guts. But there was no fuss at that time.

'Why? Because it was West Indies who were on the receiving end. There seemed to be a view in these other countries then that it didn't matter: that because we had plenty of practice in our domestic game we could handle bumpers. That is absolute rubbish.

'What has happened is that other countries, jealous of our success, have ganged up to defeat us, not fairly on the field of play but behind closed doors in the safety of their armchairs. And it won't stop until they have achieved their goal of ending our dominance'.

Understandably, since the Law governing intimidation (42-8) well defines umpires' powers regarding short-pitched bowling, a sizeable majority of county cricketers agreed with Richards that ICC's limitation— one bouncer per batsman per over—was a cop out. But it came as no surprise that no one shared his view it has been brought in to halt West Indian supremacy. ICC's method of dealing with bouncers was an artificial second best, undoubtedly; but it should have been clear enough to players of all countries that their motive was to make cricket a fairer, safer game.

Only the remarkably pure-minded or naive who have watched Test cricket outside their own country can doubt that umpires are prejudiced in favour of the home team—not all, but enough to make a difference between a fair and unfair series. In that respect England is exceptional, helped by the fact that it is the only country where enough cricket is played for former players to make a full-time job of umpiring, and thus gain the confidence to make hard decisions under pressure. The rarity with which touring teams to England request that a certain umpire should not stand in Tests—the objection of the 1953 Australians led to the quiet removal from the panel of the best-known umpire of his day, Frank Chester—pinpointed another error of the ICC in 1991, their insistence on 'neutral' umpires in all series if and when a sponsor could be found to pay the costs. Even Imran Khan of Pakistan, a vociferous long-time champion of the 'neutral umpire' concept, and with Richards the most influential Test captain of the 1980s, came round to the view that a touring team should always have the option of choosing the home country's umpires to officiate in Tests. Ironically, Pakistan might be one of the few touring teams to England not to avail themselves of such a concession, following the Test and County Cricket Board's far-reaching refusal to take David Constant off the panel at Pakistan's request in 1987.

There were two main reasons for the 1932/33 Bodyline rumpus—first because it burst upon cricket when it did, and second as a consequence of England's field-placings, which consisted of up to seven men on the legside, four or five of them close in to snaffle miscues and thick edges from batsmen warding off in self-defence waist- and chest-high balls deliberately bowled at them by a bowler of Larwood's extraordinary accuracy. That behind the arc of short-legs would lurk an outer ring of deep fielders, at long-leg, deep backward square and deep midwicket, made it impossible to hook or pull without a high degree of risk of being caught. By any standards it was an objectionable way to play the game, and by the standards of the 1930s it was shocking and outrageous; and within two years it was probably killed off by an amendment to the law.

That the bowling-system came into being and was developed as the tour progressed, rather than being hatched by the captain before the team left England as a way of curbing Bradman—then as now the highest scoring batsman in the history of cricket—as has many times been claimed, cannot exonerate Jardine. Bob Wyatt, who was vice-captain on that tour, was in fact the first to set a legside field, in the Australian XI-MCC game at Melbourne, a few weeks before the series—not with a view to intimidation, but, remarkably, as a means of saving runs. 'The pitch was so hard that after four or five overs there was no shine on the ball and instead of swinging it away, Larwood's stock delivery was coming in to the right-handers,' Wyatt recalled. 'He started the innings with four slips, but one by one I moved them to the legside to check the flow of runs, which were beginning to come freely.'

According to Wyatt, who may have turned 90 but had the advantage of being on the spot, Larwood did not bowl with legside fields in either innings of the first Test, at Sydney, where he took five for 96 and five for 28, England winning by 10 wickets. Bodyline—it always remained 'leg-theory' to the tourists—started at Melbourne, where because of the tremendous pace of the pitch on which MCC had played the Australian XI, Hedley Verity, the left-arm spinner, was dropped to make room for a fourth fast bowler, fellow-Yorkshireman Bill Bowes. In the event, all the pace had been taken out of the pitch, and as a run-saving measure in a low-scoring match Jardine, once the shine had gone, set six fielders on the leg to Larwood to restrict the batsmen's scoring options. 'Though Australia squared the rubber with a 111-run victory, Jardine's tactics were correct in those conditions,' Wyatt commented.

It was the third Test, at Adelaide, that first inflamed the crowds. Larwood, bowling to a slip field, beat Bill Woodfull, the Australian captain, with the new ball and hit him over the heart—what might be called an orthodox cricketing knock. But then, after Woodfull had recovered well enough to go on batting following treatment on the field, Jardine for the next ball switched Larwood's field and told him to bowl 'leg theory'. Tactically, a good case could be made for that as an attritional method of bowling in pre-war Australian conditions. But only a man capable of real hatred could have done anything as tactless and insensitive as switching Larwood's field against an opponent who minutes before had been lying stricken on the ground.

Wyatt had been, and remained, a close friend of Jardine's until his death in 1958, aged 57. 'He had a ruthless streak, and an intense dislike of Australians from the 1928/29 tour. Rockley Wilson, who toured Australia in 1920/21 and had taught Douglas at Winchester, said only half in jest when he was made captain that England 'might win a rubber but lose a Dominion', and he was nearly proved correct. 'But he was a staunch and kind friend and unobtrusively generous to people needing help. A proper gent.'

For reasons which none of his contemporaries was able to explain, Jardine seems to have treated the majority of Australians with withering contempt, as though he was dealing with a species of sub-race. They loathed him back, and understandably. I take Wyatt's word for it that to his friends he was delightful; but to Australian crowds, and no doubt a good few more in northern England, by far the simplest interpretation of his Harlequin cap and haughty features was that Mr. D.R. Jardine of Winchester and Oxford University was stuck-up prig. Fifteen years after Bodyline, when the first book I read about the series fanned my interest in Test cricket, the received wisdom was that Jardine's antipathy to Australians dated from 1921, when Warwick Armstrong, the tourists' captain, denied him a probable hundred for Oxford by taking so long bowling what should have been the penultimate over of the match that it became the last: Jardine, stranded at the bowler's end, finished 96 not out. A few months before he died I met him for the only time, a daunting figure still, after a bibulous cricket dinner at The Wig and Pen in Fleet Street. Dutch-couraged, I stumbled through the story and asked if it was true. 'I'm sorry,' he said frostily, looking down his nose, 'but I haven't the least idea what you're talking about.' I had enough port on board to laugh; but the way he said it made it clear why the Aussies hadn't taken to him greatly, especially when he sniffed and turned disdainfully away.

The stability of England between the end of World War One and the start of World War Two was astonishing on certain levels. In an interview he gave me on his 80th birthday, the late Les Ames, England's wicketkeeper on the Jardine tour, said the wages he was paid by Kent did not change from the time he won his county cap in 1927 until 1939. The numbers on the bank-notes may have increased a bit in 1945, but it was not until the 1950s the game itself began to change. It was so gradual that most players were unaware it was even happening. But Ken Graveney, Tom's elder brother, was in a unique position to pass judgment.

Having joined Gloucestershire in 1947, and two years later gone on to win his cap, he had not played, and seldom watched, since being forced out with a back injury in 1951. Twelve years later, aged 38, answering an SOS, he returned to captain them. 'It was extraordinary, like stepping into an unknown world,' he said. 'When I left it was a friendly game in the middle and a hard one in the dressing-room—as a young player you kept your mouth shut unless someone talked to you. One was very much aware that there were varying strata of professionals—and of course amateurs—in every side. By 1963 it had completely turned around, on the field much more grim and efficient than it was before. But the new toughness fostered team spirit, and led to friendlier relationships off-field. It had to—it was the only place the players could relax!'

Tough, yes, but with few exceptions played scrupulously fair. Batsmen who failed to save umpires difficult decisions by 'walking' were so heartily despised that from time to time one would set off when he thought he MIGHT have got an edge, just to stop accusing tongues from wagging. And such 'sledging' as went on, which tended to be merely cross-talk between fielders within the batsman's hearing, often had a veneer of humour any-way. If it wasn't Colin Cowdrey himself, it was a contemporary of his at Oxford who recounted with apparent pride that while he was preparing to face Yorkshire's England spinner Johnny Wardle in the Parks, the wicketkeeper called: 'Don't get him out for a minute or two, John—'e smells so bloody lovely!'

By the time Ken Graveney took guard for the second time in 1963, the one recorded instance of nasty sledging of which I am aware appeared in the late Sir Frank Worrell's 'Cricket Punch', his account of the 1957 West Indies tour of England. What follows is an extract from his description of the last day of their game with Surrey at the Oval, where to facilitate his team's journey to play Glamorgan at Swansea the next day, Peter May had left the tourists 320 minutes to score 270 to win.

Early in the innings, Nyron Asgarali, one of their openers, was given 'benefit of doubt' on a catch all the close fielders were convinced was out, prompting Worrell to write: 'From that moment onwards, the Surrey players kept up a constant stream of belly-aching. The objects of the belly-aching were the batsman and the umpires . . . throughout the innings we had to put up with this barracking from the Surrey players. We were abused while the players were changing ends . . . the incessant talking even went on among the close fielders while the bowler was running up to bowl. The Surrey players appealed for anything and everything. True, Peter May tried to pull his side together, and more than once told his men to 'steady on.' But the captain who handles the England side so well did not appear to get the same response from his own county on this occasion. We all got the impression Surrey wanted to be appellants, judges and jury in their own cases. The whole West Indian party was shattered by the experience. We never knew cricket could be played like that. Judging by the way they played us, Surrey are no longer capable of playing the game to enjoy it.'

In fairness to the Surrey side, who were on their way to their sixth successive Championship and included all their Test players, I must record that when I asked Micky Stewart for confirmation of the Worrell version, he vigorously denied it. 'It is a gross exaggeration. Only one fielder was involved. Asgarali refused to walk when he was clearly caught—and it happened in an era, remember, when non-walkers in county cricket were hauled up before the skipper and threatened with suspension.'

Television commentator and journalist Jack Bannister, whose Warwickshire career ended in 1968, listed one-day cricket among the causes of declining standards. 'In a 28-match county championship, which was all we played up to 1963, you might have four or five cliff-hangers a season, when the cricket got very competitive. Now, with a minimum of 21 one-day games, there might be 12 or more tight finishes, each one building up tension. Standards have declined, for a combination of factors in my opinion—fiercer competition, prize money, and overseas players coming into the game, which was when walking started to become the exception rather than the rule. I'm not blaming them for that—it just wasn't how they played the game at home. The advent of the John Player League in 1969 was another watershed—all of a sudden teams were driving away on Saturday nights to play different opponents on the Sunday instead of staying for a drink at close of play. Gradually the freemasonry of the first-class game eroded: we made more friends among the opposition than players do today.'

Sledging, in the form we know it now, began in Ray Illingworth's opinion on the Australian tour of England under Ian Chappell in 1972. 'I first encountered it as captain of the MCC team which they played at Lord's. There was nothing personal in it at that stage, in fact I burst out laughing when John Inverarity, who never swore, gave me a volley when an edge off his bowling didn't go to hand. I told him: 'Oh, no, not you too John—it doesn't suit you!' But it might have worsened that season if after the game I hadn't gone to Billy Griffith, the MCC secretary, and told him about the language that went on so that he would know England hadn't started it if it became an issue in the Tests. It turned out he knew already—the umpires had reported it.'

Inverarity, who successfully combined schoolmastering and cricket to the extent of playing six Tests for Australia, and becoming a headmaster of one of the leading schools in Western Australia, told me: 'As a schoolmaster, I believe in the mirror-of-society theory. Around the time sledging was coming in to cricket, I was teaching at a fee-paying school in Perth, day and boarding, Australia's equivalent of an English public school, in which the 16- and 17-year-olds staged a strike, refusing to come to class, when they were told to get their hair cut. It was the same the world over, a period of anti-authoritarianism, student rebellions in Paris and America, kids telling teachers to get stuffed, all that sort of thing.

'I think the connection is underplayed about what goes on outside—the early 1970s were most difficult years for people in authority, and the time when cricket manners coarsened. I have no collection of swearing at Ray Illingworth at Lord's—it's unlikely because I hardly ever hit the edge!—but I could have. By 1972 sledging was our accepted way of playing. Tony Greig had plenty to say too, but I'm sure the Aussies were the main offenders.'

At a range of many years, Alvin Kallicharran, the little Guyanese left-hander who finished his career with Warwickshire, looks back with something approaching amusement on Greig's sledging on MCC's tour of the West Indies under Mike Denness in 1973/74. 'It was very racial—you little black this and you little black that and I was near the start of my career. It made me uncomfortable and I didn't like it. But things were going my way—I made 158 in the first Test and 93 in the second, and then another hundred in the third—and all the time this stuff was going on around me. Then Donald Carr, the MCC manager, got wind of it, and ordered Greig to stop. At Georgetown and Port of Spain, in the final Test which England won, I battled in an eerie silence and got six and then a pair of noughts!'

A long time after the event, even sledging produces the odd macabre laugh. But as part of a team's strategy it is contemptible. It saddens me that cricketers of the fame and stature of Bob Simpson and Allan Border, Australia's team manager and captain, should condone and practice it. If the 1991 Code of Conduct stamps sledging out, it will have served its purpose. Again, though, it must be said that, had umpires done their job, it might have been a nine-day wonder. Indeed, most of the things that sully cricket would vanish in a year if sections 1 and 2 of Law 42 (Unfair Play) were observed. '1. The captains are responsible at all times for ensuring that play is conducted within the spirit of the game as well as within the Laws. 2. The umpires are the sole judges of fair and unfair play.' On England's 1990/91 tour of Australia, suggestions were occasionally made to England batsmen about what their wives or girl friends might be getting up to in their absence that would have been best answered by a knee in the groin. All old stuff, repetitive and puerile, which over the years cricketers have had to learn to live with—Jeff Dujon, the West Indies wicketkeeper, goes so far as to say that in his view no batsman can regard himself as proven at Test level until he had shown the ability to bat through sledging. But 'fair play'? Pathetically, by their lack of intervention, umpires seem to think so.

Umpires are coming badly out of this and I regret that because it is the most demanding job in cricket, made all the harder by TV replays. But that firmness is effective is indisputable as the following example shows.

On England's 1974/75 tour of Australia, the one on which Dennis Lillee and Jeff Thomson forged their frighteningly effective bowling partnership, the most dramatic Test was the fourth at Sydney. Played on a fast uneven pitch in front of crowds that chanted Lillee's name expectantly whenever he came on to bowl, it was the match in which John Edrich took over the England captaincy from Mike Denness, who dropped himself, and narrowly failed to stop Australia winning back the Ashes when he returned to bat with broken ribs (by Lillee) and made a fighting 33 not out in 2¼ hours. There were a lot of other bumps and bruises because of the pitch's inconsistency, among them one that might have been much more serious than it was when a flier from Thomson ricocheted off Keith Fletcher's gloves onto his cap and carried to within a yard of Ross Edwards's forward plunge at cover.

Lillee also got a thump, from a bouncer by Geoff Arnold, and it had a sequel that showed the benefits of firm umpiring. When it was Arnold's turn to bat, Lillee greeted him with one of the fastest and most dangerous balls ever bowled. Fired in with every ounce of Lillee's strength and venom, it whistled past Arnold's head, cleared Rod Marsh 20 yards behind the stumps, and clattered into the sightscreen second bounce after leaving the fast bowler's hand. 'That's your ration to Arnold, Dennis,' said umpire Tom Brooks as Lillee walked past him to his mark. 'Like hell it is, Tom, I've only just started on him!' Lillee grinned maliciously. 'No, Dennis. It's the start and it's the finish, and that's final,' Brooks called sternly. Umpires complain that they do not always get sufficient backing at Board level. They may have a point on some issues. But it is as least as likely they if they showed the strength Brooks displayed to Lillee, another of the game's problems would be solved.

Boards of Control, however, outranking umpires, have as much or more to answer for. Knowing the character of Haseeb Ahsan, manager of the 1987 Pakistanis, the Test and County Cricket Board should have been able to anticipate the viper's nest they were stirring up in blocking his request to take Constant off the panel—the first paving stone on the road to Mike Gatting's very public hell as Faisalabad. And that balanced judge Richie Benaud is scathing in his criticism of the Australian Cricket Board over their leniency to Lillee following his notorious scuffle with Javed Miandad during Australia's 1981/82 Test against Pakistan at Perth.

Lillee was the equal of any fast bowler since World War Two, but possibly also the most volatile. Of the bowlers to take 300 Test Wickets, only Malcolm Marshall, Richard Hadlee and Fred Trueman bettered his average of 23.92, and none his striking-rate of 5.07 wickets per Test—355 in

70 in all. The hostility that was part of his make-up as a bowler, though, stemmed from a temper that often seemed close to boiling-point when luck was against him, and his loss of it at Perth, gave rise to a photograph that presented cricket in a light in which it had never been seen before—a street brawl manqué featuring a Test umpire pushing his way between a bowler and a batsman to stop them assaulting one another.

Miandad, being small, agile, cocky, and not least a member of the team with the worst reputation for sportsmanship in cricket, fulfilled all the criteria needed to get under Lillee's skin. In the course of scoring 79 the Pakistan captain's opportunities for needling the opposition would have been plentiful, and Lillee's temper snapped. As Miandad was running a routine single for a push on the onside, Lillee side-stepped two paces to block him. Rather than swerve round him, Miandad held his course, knocking Lillee aside, and reached his crease as the bowler turned and launched a kick at him. Though it all happened in seconds, the umpire, Tony Crafter, quickly put himself between them as Miandad swung his bat in which he claimed was self-defence, but looked (1983 Wisden picture section) more like naked aggression.

There were wrongs on both sides. Irritating opponents was part of Miandad's stock in trade. But on the occasion there was no question Lillee was to blame. Yet if the A.C.B. had not suspended him for two matches following a protest by the umpires, he would have escaped with a fine of 200 Australian dollars—less than £100! Benaud commented: 'The quaint aspect of that was that he was suspended for two one-day matches though the kicking had been done in a Test.

'I haven't changed my mind from what I wrote at the time. 'The penalty imposed was far too light. It should have been 2,000 Australian dollars and a two-*Test* match suspension, and a statement should have been issued that future transgressions by any other Australian player would mean a fine of 4,000 Australian dollars and four Tests, and the next one 8,000 and eight Tests. You would put a stop to that sort of nonsense inside one season.'

'In 1991 I would still use the same system,' Benaud added, 'automatic doubling of an initial penalty until the players realised they were on a losing proposition.

'More recently, the 1990/91 Australian tour of the West Indies, produced confrontations on the field, some of them more childish than dangerous and often geared towards television. Don't think, though, that the modern-day players have introduced something entirely new to the game. In his wonderful book, 'Cricket, a Social History', John Ford makes the point that cricket is a mirror of society. It always has been. That may be unfortunate, but what he says is true and has been since the first Test was played in 1877.'

If Gatting's spitting match with Shakoor Rana at Faisalabad caused even greater ructions, it stemmed from the fact that it directly concerned an umpire. In isolation, the 30-second clip of England's captain sticking a forefinger in Rana's face was damning. On the small screen it looked disgraceful; judged by the accepted conventions of cricket, it was unforgivable. No captain should ever lose his temper, especially the captain of a touring team in a Third World country.

It was significant, though, that whereas Gatting was almost universally condemned by people seeing the incident on film, all but one member of the British media watching 'live', and knowing the provocation Gatting was under, took a different view. Rana was the catalyst. But the incident was set in train by Shakil Khan, whose umpiring in the Lahore Test a week before took away what remote chance England had against Abdul Qadir on a crumbling, grassless pitch which was in use for the second time that month. Opinion varied in the touring team whether Shakil Khan had made six, seven, eight or nine erroneous decisions in favour of the Pakistan bowlers— the hapless David Capel bagged a pair, both 'caught', without laying bat on ball in either knock. What was indisputable was that Shakil Khan's performance contravened Law 3 of cricket, whose first clause reads: 'Before the toss two umpires shall be appointed, one for each end, to control the game with absolute impartiality as required by the Laws.'

To understand Gatting's rage at Faisalabad it was necessary to know not only what had happened at Lahore, but of the timing of the incident and the lack of justification for Shakoor Rana's intervention. In an effort to squeeze in an extra over on the second evening, with Pakistan hanging on at 106 for five in reply to England's 292, Gatting brought Capel in from deep square-leg to a position in the single-saving zone, in order to hasten the change-round between overs. Though he was under no obligation to do so he alerted the striker, Salim Malik, to the switch, which was made after four balls of an over by Eddie Hemmings, England's offspinner, about 90 seconds before the close of play. As Hemmings was in the act of delivering the fifth ball, Gatting, seeing Capel approaching closer than he wanted, gestured him to stop as he estimated his distance from the bat out of the corner of his eye from his own position at short-leg.

At this Shakoor Rana intervened, loudly enough for the umpire at the bowler's end, Khizar Hayat, to call 'dead ball' with the delivery from Hemmings in the air. Fielders within earshot claimed that in causing play to stop, Rana accused Gatting of being a 'f****** cheating c***'. Gatting's immediate and almost violent reaction certainly implied some such phrase was used. There were wrongs on both sides, undeniably: but after Shakil Khan's shameless umpiring at Lahore, and Shakoor Rana's own at Faisalabad, where he gave Graham Gooch out caught when his bat was at no stage within six inches of the ball, to be accused of cheating was the final straw. Had England's management thought of it, they could have warmly recommended in return a closer adherence to Law 3.

Imran Khan's recognition that mistrust of umpires was at the root of a high proportion of the dissent, and manic appealing, that disfigured an increasing number of Tests in the 1970s and 1980s, was a big factor in John Hampshire and John Holder, who was Barbados-born but domiciled in England since his 20s, umpiring Pakistan's home series against India 1989/90. It worked better than even Imran had imagined. Wisden reported: 'Two cricketers made a quiet and yet very effective contribution to the tenth series between India and Pakistan. They were not players. John Hampshire and John Holder, both from England, were the 'third country' umpires invited to officiate in the four Test matches, and their presence changed the nature of the contest between these two Asian neighbours. The frisson was missing. Events on the field were far less contentious, with both teams accepting the umpires, and their rulings, in good faith. The occasional mistakes, some of them glaring, did not lead to flare-ups, with the result that the atmosphere was refreshingly free from suspicion. Teams had been touring Pakistan for years without any firm belief that they could, or even would be allowed to, win a Test. In this series, the relations between the team was cordial and the cricket, if not spectacular, was highly competitive.'

How different the visit of the West Indies to New Zealand 10 years earlier, the series in which as a direct consequence of the disaffection of Clive Lloyd's team with the umpires, Wisden recorded that a public 'which had looked forward keenly to the West Indian's visit, was glad to see the back of them.' That was the series in which Michael Holding, having had an appeal for a catch at the wicket refused, ran the length of the pitch to send the stumps flying with a full-blooded kick alongside Gatting's nose-to-nose with Shakoor Rana cricket's most vivid picture of dissent. (1981 Wisden, p.67). 'At Christchurch in the second Test,' continued Wisden, 'Croft, after being no-balled, flicking off the bails as he walked back, and a little later ran in very close to the umpire, F.R. Goodall—so close that the batsman could not see him—and shouldered Goodall heavily. It was the height of discourtesy when Goodall, wishing on two occasions to talk to Lloyd about Croft's behaviour, had to walk all the way to the West Indian captain, standing deep in the slips. Lloyd did not take a step to meet him.'

It was no coincidence that West Indies tour took place within two years of Kerry Packer's brief and shattering intrusion into the until then cloistered world of cricket. In certain respects—the game's marketability, players' salaries, night cricket—World Series Cricket gave the game a jolt it badly needed. But the effect was brutalising too.

Have no doubt of the provocation cricketers are subjected to, and not only by the opposition or the umpires. In his book 'The Art of Captaincy', Mike Brearley tells how his criticism of Geoff Boycott for signing autographs on the boundary at Melbourne softened into sympathy when he learned that England's outfielders were being bombarded by 're-filled' beer cans. 'When I realised just how nasty spectators could be,' he wrote, 'I saw that appeasement was undoubtedly not a bad bet,' adding: 'After some unsavory episodes, the authorities restricted cans per spectator to . . . 24!'

Under Mike Gatting on the second leg of the Shakoor Rana tour, England's dissent against New Zealand's admittedly sub-standard umpiring was no less blatant than West Indies', and in the sense that they were under orders after Pakistan to accept decisions without demur however bad they were, little less disgraceful. On three occasions, two concerning Martin Crowe, England's attitudes of incredulous disbelief brought the game to a standstill when New Zealand's best batsman was adjudged 'not out' after edging the ball so palpably they were expecting him to walk. It was the firmness of the contact, it emerged, that most irritated the fielders—they considered it an insult to the umpire for Crowe to wait for a decision. It was as telling an example as I have encountered of the hypocrisy of cricketers: follow that line of thinking to its logical conclusion and you find that the thinner the contact, the more 'right' a batsman has to stay—the very situation in which the true sportsman would save an umpire a possible mistake by walking out unbidden.

The roll of dishonour has an extra entry almost every year—John Snow barging over Sunil Gavaskar at Lord's, Keith Fletcher as England captain flicking his stumps askew on being given out at Bangalore, Greg Chappell instructing his brother Trevor to bowl a sneak underarm delivery on the last ball of a match to stop New Zealand's No. 10 hitting six to tie at Melbourne, Geoff Boycott throwing his bat down at Adelaide, Lillee his— the aluminium one—at Perth. Just to name a few.

Nobody following the game would say that, in spirit, it had gone anything but backwards since the 1960s. Lillee, the Chappells, Lloyd, Holding, Croft, Richards, Greig, Gatting, Miandad and many, many others less dramatically—have all done things which, when they thought about them privately, should have made them cringe, and with any luck still do.

But for sheer unscrupulousness, nothing I have heard of can touch a scene that was enacted when World War Two was still a recent memory. Before tossing for innings in big games became a ritual, with TV cameras, commentators and officials straining to get in on the act, two Test captains walked out together on a ground renowned for the perfection of its batting conditions. The toss was a formality: when the visiting captain guessed wrong, his host shook hands with him, shrugging sympathetically, retrieved the coin, and walked beside him back to the pavilion.

And 10 yards from the gate his opponent turned and softly said: 'We'll bat.' What could the home captain do—capitulate or cause a diplomatic incident? Twenty minutes later, tight lipped, he led his team into the field.

ADDENDA: CODE OF CONDUCT

1. The captains are responsible at all times for ensuring that play is conducted within the spirit of the game as well as within the laws.

2. Players and team officials shall not at any time engage in conduct unbecoming to an international player or team official which could bring the game into disrepute.

3. Players and team officials must at all times accept the umpire's decision. Players must not show dissent at the umpire's decision.

4. Players and team officials shall not intimidate, assault or attempt to intimidate or assault an umpire, another player or a spectator.

5. Players and team officials shall not use crude or abusive language (known as 'sledging') nor make offensive gestures.

6. Players and team officials shall not use or in any way be concerned in the distribution of illegal drugs.

7. Players and team officials shall not disclose or comment upon any alleged breach of the code or upon any hearing, report or decision arising from such breach.

8. Players and team officials shall not make any public pronouncement or media comment which is detrimental either to the game in general; or to a particular tour in which they are involved; or about any tour between other countries which is taking place; or to relations between the boards of the competing teams.

GOLF

Renton Laidlaw

Human nature being what it is and human beings what they are it would be wrong to suggest that golf was devoid of spiteful behaviour of one kind or another. It is not but the Royal and Ancient game can also claim to have a very special characteristic compared to many other sports, especially the team sports. Everyone is duty bound to play by the rules.

Those who play it at the top level in the amateur game and at professional level jealously guard the game's hard-earned reputation for sportsmanship and fair-play. Because of this, there is no golfing equivalent of the professional foul. Maybe because it is not a contact sport that is understandable. The fact is that in few sports is the contestant his own referee. In amateur events and, except in majors and pro events such as the Ryder Cup, the golfer himself has the responsibility most other sportsmen and sportswomen do not have or, dare I say, necessarily want.

In short, golf is a game of trust. Break the rules and you let yourself down. Do it regularly and you are quickly ex-communicated. You are booted out of the club or kicked off whatever pro Tour you happen to be playing. There is no place in the game for the golfer who makes a habit of replacing his ball at a point ahead of his marker and nearer the hole by some shrewd sleight of hand. There is no room for the 'leather-mashie' man whose deft footwork effectively improves the lie of the ball. They will be found out.

No matter how hard their opponents are concentrating they will be caught eventually just like David Robertson was in the 1985 Open Championship qualifying at Princes. He was proved to have been moving the ball several feet nearer the hole hoping to take advantage of the fact that the other two golfers in the group would be concentrating so hard on their own games that they would not notice that he had casually flicked his marker nearer the hole when he had picked up the ball to clean it before putting and therefore returned it to a different spot on the green. Curiously, sometimes a player will try to gain an advantage of just an inch or so—not much but psychologically huge! Robertson was accused of gaining feet! Graeme Simmers, who went on to run the Open Championship with all the responsibilities that entails, was the official in charge at that 1985 qualifying when Robertson, a former Scottish amateur international and player of considerable talent, was caught, disqualified and later fined £5,000 and banned by the P.G.A. European Tour for 20 years. There was no appeal. Robertson realised the game was up and accepted his punishment severe enough to deter others from trying to do the same.

Cases like this are rare but do happen. The authorities, especially in the professional game, have a tendency to deal with such issues in camera. No one gets away with cheating but when a culprit is caught and sentenced it is not always announced. Professional bodies like to maintain the reputation of the game by saying nothing. They might argue they have their finger on anyone stepping out of line but since cheating is against all the principles around which the game is built perhaps they should be more public about it. Dealing with the golfer who plays 'jumping bean' with his marker or who breaks the rules in some other way, maybe even going so far as have his caddie have another ball of similar make and number ready to slip through a hole in the pocket of his trousers and into play if the original should not be found, deserves to be publicly pilloried!

Tom Watson, five times Open champion and in modern times one of golf's genuine giants until his putting deserted him, says: 'You can cheat if you want but in your heart you will know that you cheated and who wants to go through life aware he is a cheat?' Some people do, blocking out of their mind the fact that they are cheating at all. Watson has himself been involved in incidents regarding the rules notably a famous occasion with Gary Player in one of those end of season Skins games played out for television at a resort course in America for ludicrously inflated prize-money.

The matter became a cause célèbre. Watson claimed that Player had improved the lie behind his ball at one hole by 'repositioning' a live weed that was growing behind it—a clear infringement of the rules. Only non-growing, unattached objects may be removed. Nothing was said at the time and nothing might have been said because of the difficulty in this case of proving it, but a journalist from the New York Times, not eaves-dropping but passing by at a time when Watson was speaking to a rules official about his fears of an infringement, ran the story the following day. Watson remained adamant in his view that Player had broken a rule. Gary was incensed. He denied it but went further questioning why if Watson thought he had slipped up, he had not said anything at the time. To this day the two are coldly distant. Significantly, Tom Watson never did accept any of the invitations sent out to play the Sun City Million Dollar Challenge at Bophuthatswana where Player was pro and had built the course. Neither player came out well in the affair; Watson should have spoken up sooner or kept quiet about it. His crime was in letting Player get away with it if he really felt something wrong had been done. It still wrankles Player so much he brought the incident up in a recent book he wrote. He claims to this day that he was unfairly and wrongfully accused but there has been no spiteful repercussion by Player to the sad affair.

Watson himself was caught out by the rules in, of all things, the Tournament of Champions played at Carlsbaad in Southern California one year. As he and Lee Trevino walked from a green on the back nine to the next tee along a path, their conversation, innocent enough, was being picked up on one of the microphones being used by the television company covering the event. As luck would have it, the producer at that moment had no other action to go to. He stayed with Trevino and Watson and, for once, the American commentators, noted for their wall-to-wall commentating style, actually stayed silent. Imagine the shock with which officials heard the two friends discuss this, that and suddenly Trevino's form! 'Know what your doing wrong,' said Watson going into an explanation of why Trevino was either hooking or slicing shots. All hell was let loose.

There was nothing wrong with the advice Watson had given Trevino but under the rules Trevino could not accept any advice, no matter how casually or matter-of-factly given and Trevino could not give it. There was nothing spiteful about Watson's action it was just a genuine slip-up. Watson was leading the tournament but would as a result of his misguided helpfulness, given in the spur of the moment and with no thought of rules breaking, have to be penalised two shots. Fortunately the five times Open champion ended up with a three-shot advantage over the field so the penalty did not make any difference to the final result. Watson still took first prize but it highlighted how easy it is to break the rules of golf and why the authorities are so much on top of those who, unlike Trevino or Watson, do so with 'malice of fore-thought'.

Of course issues regarding the rules cause hours of discussion in the bar after a round is over. Who was right in this incident or that? Was the rule unfair and should it be changed? In equity was the wrong fellow penalised? Sometimes the rules queries that crop up can be positively bizarre! In America during a women's team match a player hit her ball into a bunker. When she stepped in to play her shot she spotted a rattlesnake just a few inches from her ball . . . and promptly stepped out again. What should she do? Her opponent, clearly a tough old contestant who knew the rules backwards—and it is a curious fact that women usually do and use them more effectively—insisted that the woman, unable to remove loose impediments from the bunker, had no option but to play the ball as it lay or concede the hole. Then, as a special concession, she offered to stand close by with a rake which she would use to club the snake if it attacked her opponent! Yet is a snake a loose impediment? Is it not an outside agency in golfing terms and therefore capable of being gingerly removed without penalty? The discussion continued. There was another solution and that was for the woman whose ball was in the bunker to use her sand-wedge to kill the snake before playing her shot with the same club but cold water was thrown on this by the woman's opponent who hinted that in the process of killing the snake the unfortunate lady whose ball was in the bunker could be deemed to be testing the sand and thereby incurring a further rules infringement. I believe the woman in the bunker took the easy and most sensible option open to her by conceding the hole to an opponent who might have been considered in the context of this book as spiteful.

Still if it should happen to you the United States Golf Association, later asked to adjudicate on the matter, came down on the side of common sense. No player should be asked to hit a shot from such a dangerous situation. The solution should have been for the player involved to have dropped another ball in another bunker, no nearer the hole and in as similar a lie as possible without penalty!

Playing golf was never meant to endanger life which is why, on reflection, the committee at a course in South-east Asia were exceptionally hard on two competitors recently. In an area where tigers, monkeys, six-foot long lizards and huge pythons prompt competitors to keep their eyes open and themselves in a fair state of fitness for the sudden dash to the safety of the clubhouse, these two golfers discovered, when they came to the tee at the 17th., that it was occupied—not by the group ahead but by a small herd of wild-looking water buffaloes with fierce looking horns and a 'move us at your peril' look in their eyes. Discretion being the better part of valour, the two contestants played off a slightly forward tee using, it would have to be said, a faster than normal swing. Laughing about it in the clubhouse later within ear-shot of the competition organiser, they were quickly disqualified for not having played the full length of the course by some 20 yards. All legal and above board but the organiser surely lacked a sense of humour and a certain sensitivity. Maybe he was just getting his own back on one of the contestants out of sheer spite.

These days with television coverage of golf so widespread the golfers have been faced with a new phenomenon—the armchair referee, the viewer at home who thinks he saw a rules infringement and cannot wait to report it—either by phoning the headquarters of the U.S. P.G.A. Tour or the host club. This was the case in the Watson—Trevino incident.

In the 1991 U.S.P.G.A. Championship, for instance, John Daly, the broad-shouldered blond-haired giant of a man who went on to win the title, came off the green at the end of the third round with what he thought was a three-shot lead. His delight was not, however, immediately apparent as he was swept off by P.G.A. officials to view the video tape of what had happened to him on the 12th. green. He had had long putt there which was going to break sharply to the right. Unfortunately his caddie could be seen clearly, pin in hand with the base of it touching the grass. Now this is not allowed. The caddie may indicate the line but without touching the grass in the process. You may have seen them pointing out the preferred route for the ball with the tip of their finger or the tip of the flag but always an inch or two above the ground. The question was simply whether or not the caddie was indicating the line or not. If he was he would incur a two shot penalty for the man he was working for. Daly's lead would be cut to just one with a round to go if that were the case. The tape was viewed several times before the P.G.A. of America ruled that the caddie was not, in this instance, indicating the line and that although he was technically touching the grass there would be no penalty.

An anxious moment for Daly ended happily, more happily than it did for moustachioed Craig Stadler, whose nickname 'The Walrus' seems so appropriate. No one could argue that Stadler would ever challenge Nick Faldo in the fashion stakes but Craig has his standards and when required to play a shot from beneath a bush in the 1987 San Diego Open at Torrey Pines he knew he would have to kneel down and play the kind of trick shot that Noel Hunt makes such a fine living at in his one-man show. Careful as ever, Stadler decided that in order not to dirty his trousers he would lay down, on the dirty ground, the towel his caddie carried to clean the golf balls from time to time. What Stadler did not realise, but several viewers watching on television but saying nothing until the following day did, was that there was a golf ruling which indicated that anyone kneeling on a towel to play a shot was breaching Rule 13-3 which does not allow a player to build a stance! Daft, you might think but the decision was based on the rule that prevents anyone carrying a mat on which to stand to play shots. Of course, if you happen to be playing on one of those desert courses in places such as Dubai a mat is essential equipment not to stand on but to put the ball on if you are on the staked-out designated fairway of an all sand course. Stadler was not in the desert and, Tour officials were obliged to take action on the public reporting of a possible infringement. The Walrus was disqualified for not having included the penalty in the score he had signed for a day earlier. This prompted a shoal of letters to the Tour from other members of the public emphasising how unfair they thought the ruling had been. The situation was given a high profile that year because Stadler would have finished tied second had he been prepared to get his trousers dirty.

There was as much concern about the fairness of that decision as there was in 1968 at Augusta when that Argentinian gentleman of golf Roberto de Vicenzo was disqualified for signing for the wrong score put down on his card by Tommy Aaron. Millions of viewers watched as De Vicenzo, the gentlest and most gracious of men, took 3 at the par 4 17th. Then parred the last to tie Bob Goalby. The South American thus missed the play-off by a shot.

Tom Kite, the top American golfer who has never landed a major title despite winning more prize money than anyone else on the U.S. Tour—he is currently chasing his seventh million—has had an award for sportsmanship bestowed upon him for doing nothing more dramatic than sticking to the rules . . . but in unusual circumstances. He was in contention to win a 1978 tournament when, unbeknown to anyone but himself, the ball moved after he had grounded his putter but just before he putted. No one saw the incident and even the ever-vigilant television lens was not recording the scene in close-up when the incident occurred. He called the shot on himself immediately, lost the chance of a lucrative first prize and was presented with the Bobby Jones award for sportsmanship. Jones has been the role model regarding sportsmanship for so many golfers, not least Jack Nicklaus. The legendary Georgian noted for his total commitment to fair play throughout his relatively short competitive career, set behavioural standards which are religiously followed today. Yet can the game of golf be as clean as it purports to be?

Surely there are occasions when golfers, without breaking any rules, behave in a dubious manner in order to gain a vital edge on his or her opponent? How often does a naturally slow and deliberate player become even more slow and deliberate when playing against an opponent he knows enjoys playing quickly and who hates hanging around waiting to hit every shot? That may not be spiteful but it does come into the category of gamesmanship and there is a place for that in any sport as long as it does not develop into sheer bloody-mindedness.

Mind you Tommy Horton, one of golf's most experienced professionals, can recall a certain amount of spite being shown by some of the older fellows when he first turned pro. Years ago when the European Tour was only a British and Irish circuit and did not zig-zag its way through Europe like the Volvo Tour does today, the older pros — or some of them at least— did not like it when younger, fitter, more enthusiastic golfers came along to upset their cosy tournament scene . . . and made no secret, in some cases, of showing their displeasure. Horton recalls turning up on one first tee to play with someone who, for propriety's sake he prefers not to identify. He was a big name at the time and Horton was excited to be playing with him. When they shook hands on the tee, somewhat grudgingly on the older man's behalf but strictly according to golfing etiquette, Horton was astonished to hear the older fellow say: 'I've heard you're quite good but I also hear your swing is a bit suspect. I shall be watching you very carefully all the way round . . . remember that.' It was an intimidating comment which the youthful Horton found difficult to stomach. He did not score well.

On another occasion the young Horton playing with a former Open champion whose competitiveness was always razor-sharp, was surprised when, having holed a few putts, he was asked by his more experience rival: 'This your birthday then?' Horton replied innocently enough that it was not although curious to find out what had prompted the unusual question. He soon found out why. 'God almighty I thought it had to be the way your holing all those putts. You cannot keep on doing that,' said the senior pro sourly. Horton remonstrated mildly at the unfairness of the remarks in order to satisfy his own honour and promptly lost his putting touch for the rest of the round. Was that spiteful behaviour or gamesmanship which every professional has to learn to live with and cope with?

As recently as the 1991 Ryder Cup match at Kiawah Island Seve Ballesteros, no less, was described by Paul Azinger as 'King of Gamesmanship'—a title the Spaniard would vigorously deny. He is a great competitor and this incident has happily been forgotten by the two who are good friends.

There is a fine line, of course, between stepping completely out of line and adopting unfair questionable tactics and the subtle art (if that is the word) of gamesmanship. A colleague of mine with whom I sometimes play regularly rattles the coins in his pocket. It is disturbing but he does not do it deliberately. It is just a thoughtless act that I and others have got used to. He never would cough at the top of the backswing or practice putt when in my eye line when I was putting nor would he step on my line at any point to gain an advantage by perhaps creating a spike mark and making my putt more difficult. He would not do that but others might. An innocent enough looking scuff of the shoes close by the hole could make it much more difficult for following players to putt especially as under the rules spike marks can not be repaired until after the hole has been completed! It happens. Just as it happens that sometimes competitors do repair spike marks illegally thus cheating themselves and all their other competitors as well.

You can repair plug marks made when a ball lands but not a spike mark, as Bernard Langer found to his cost in the 29th. Ryder Cup at Kiawah Island. He had two to negotiate in the six-feet between his ball and the hole and missed the putt when the ball was deflected right of the cup. No accusation there of course of deliberate spiking up of the area around the hole by the Americans; the spike marks could have been made by an earlier colleague of Bernhard's in the European team! It was just bad luck—hard to bear but part of the game and accepted however unwillingly. The fact is that if players were allowed to repair spike marks as well as plug marks, rounds might take even longer as players went on extensive gardening expeditions in the area between their ball and the hole!

Off the course there would appear to be little indication of spitefulness between players on the professional circuits despite the fact that not all of them get on as splendidly as you might imagine with each other. How could they? Sometimes there is a natural affinity between players, other times, for one reason or another, a player dislikes another one because of his personality or his attitude, or simply the way he expresses himself and behaves. In such cases their relationship is a purely professional one and goes no further when they step off the course.

Muffin Spencer-Devlin, a lively lady whom, I understand, considers in an earlier life she was Mary Queen of Scots, has been known to make the wrong kind of headlines. She gave the tournament director a mouthful in the 1990 Ford Classic at Woburn, the complex owned by the Marquis of Tavistock. Had she done so on the course out of range of most people that would have been marginally acceptable if still wrong and open to penalty, but she had her colourfully worded outburst in public at the tournament dinner when distressed to find she had not, after all, been seated at the top table! Maybe she saw a spiteful reason for what she considered a damaging slight but she counted the cost in terms of a fine and a temporary ban, happily now lifted. Miss Spencer-Devlin, whose most spiteful action that day had been her remarks about the golfing competence of one of her pro-am partners, a journalist with a particularly pleasant personality but less than aesthetic swing, has turned over a new leaf and is now a welcome guest again wherever she chooses to play. The pressures that prompted her capturing the kind of headlines the women's Tour on either side of the Atlantic do not need were highlighted by the incident. She reminded us that even professional golfers have a human side, that they can and do sometimes blow their tops, can act in an angry and irrational way when things are going wrong. The bottom line is Muffin's doing all right now playing golf and leading the kind of life that suits her.

So is golf as clean as it is made out to be? The answer, of course, is that it is comparatively much cleaner than most other sports. The incidents of wrong doing at professional level stand out like sore thumbs because they are so unusual.

For instance take the Jack Nicklaus affair when he stupidly took on Col. Tony Duncan, the official referee assigned to his match, in the World Match-play at Wentworth one year. When he did not get the relief he felt he was entitled to but which, in all equity and honesty, Duncan knew it would have been wrong to concede, Nicklaus made an almighty fuss. He was in a not too pleasant lie in the rough and wanted relief claiming an advertising sign well ahead of him and hardly in play for the type of shot he was going to be able to hit, was in his line. Duncan assessed that taking the lie of Nicklaus' ball the sign could not have come into play but the atmosphere was so tense that Col. Duncan asked whether the Golden Bear would prefer someone else to take over. In an incident one of sport's greatest ever athletes and sportsmen will never be allowed to forget, he said he would. Duncan stood down and, I suspect to this day Nicklaus regrets not having accepted with good grace a decision arrived at by a referee who, bending over backwards to be fair, had made what he considered to be a fair ruling.

Nick Faldo's incident in the same event a few years later with Graham Marsh when a spectator kicked the twice Open champion and U.S. Master's ball back on to the 16th green when it shot through the back is another incident often recalled. It was seen by millions on television. With Faldo and Marsh, unaware of what happened, and the referee unwilling or unable to handle the situation as reported by fans around the green, the hole was won by Faldo. It was hardly his fault that justice was not seen to be done on that occasion!

And what about Graham Marsh's assertion that Gary Player played from a spot ahead of the tee at the 17th in one of their Wentworth encounters in Player's response that if he did, so, too, had Marsh because Gary had put his tee peg in the hole left by Marsh's peg! Ludicrously amusing stuff but rare incidents all in the week-in, week-out devotion to fair play and honest competition.

Paul Azinger, who was spotted by a viewer moving a pebble underwater as he took up his stance in a hazard and was later penalised or Tom Kite, who was accused of dropping in the wrong spot after hitting into a water hazard, would not argue that having inadvertently slipped up they were right to be penalised but is big brother in the shape of the television camera and the eagle-eyed viewer doing golf a service by helping maintain the proud standard of golf for sportsmanship and honesty or is it eroding the basic fundamentals of the game which puts the onus on the player to maintain and play by the rules?

At Augusta in the Masters and at the U.S. Open and Open Championships there is a referee with every group and a close monitoring is made of all television coverage in order that, as much as possible in a game that extends over 18-holes and 100 acres, as few rules are broken as possible. The reputation the game has for sportsmanship and fair play—a reputation that has helped the game grow so dramatically in recent years around the world is jealously protected. Personal spite may at times be present but the problem in golf of maliciously spiteful behaviour, while present, is thankfully very small.

HORSE RACING

Christopher Poole

The Jockey Club, British horse racing's self-electing ruling body, has controlled the Turf with Establishment poise and paternalism for more than two centuries. But now it is a deep conflict with sections of Westminster opinion and racing's progressive wing, under siege and, perhaps, in its depth throes.

The pall bearers are not as yet waiting in line on Newmarket Heath or polishing the handles of a coffin outside the elegant West End offices from which a vast sporting complex is administered but the days of well-meaning but fallible amateurs at the helm are numbered and some kind of electoral college to produce a democratic professional authority answerable to the industry itself is within vision. This fundamental shift of horse power will bring with it major changes in the way Turf discipline works.

Out should go the panels of local stewards whose unqualified opinions currently damage the sport's standing and integrity. A majority of trainers and jockeys have long since lost all faith in the system claiming, often in well-founded truth, that their livelihoods should not be subject, even in the short term, to the views of people with little or no knowledge of the crafts of preparing and riding the Thoroughbred. The replacement of such Turf illiterates by stipendary stewards' panels made up largely of former trainers and jockeys is an obvious step to improving sport's internal discipline, not to mention an advancement in standards which will benefit racegoers and off-course punters.

Horse racing, with its near-total reliance on betting, has always been vulnerable to unscrupulous acts. In company with greyhound racing, the Turf will always attract an element of unprincipled rouges on the lookout for easy money. Such characters are still found both within the sport itself and seeking to operate from the wings.

All-too-recent examples of horse doping in this country and Ireland show conclusively that this menace, putting at risk not just punters' cash but also the lives of horses and their riders, has yet to be eliminated despite the vigilance of racing's own security services and the police.

But a more widespread problem is cheating within the sport itself and, sad to relate, the Jockey Club seems quiet unable to come to grips with this unsatisfactory state of affairs. Action against those responsible for running and riding horses at less than peak merit, in other words non-triers, is haphazard and ineffectual, largely because stewarding at local level is so poor.

This type of malpractice remains widespread in British racing and it appears that the authorities, as presently constituted, are able to do little by way of counter measures. In countries where qualified professional stewards are in action—Australia and the United States are notable examples—there is almost no obvious non-trying and, I suspect, far less general saboteur activity against form book accuracy.

Scobie Breasley, one of Australia's greatest jockeys who was also British champion on four occasions during a lengthy and distinguished career in the saddle, once told me that the pre-war standard of stewarding in his native country was far superior to that found here some 30 years later. I have no reason to question his expert judgement.

Breasley puts down this discrepancy in control between two of the world's first division Turf nations to the fact that Australia has, for many years, employed professional ex-jockeys as stewards. 'Those who have race ridden regularly know what to look for,' Breasley said. 'You can't fool them one time in a hundred. And they know the form book inside out.

'But amateur stewards, most of whom have very little idea about tactics or how to ride a horse at racing pace, are all too easily fooled. I have seen British jockeys get away with things which would have had them stood down in double quick time in Australia.

'Often enough, an Australian official will just tap a jockey on the shoulder and let him know that he was spotted doing something wrong. It is a kind of behind-the-scenes warning which any rider is wise to take notice of. In England stewards are very formal but much more likely to return a wrong verdict. A lot of jockeys when I was riding had no respect for them and I expect that is still true today.'

Undoubtedly it is and the sooner radical change is introduced and full-time professional stewards are acting, the tighter and better race riding discipline in this country will become.

That particular racing problem is, in my view, solvable if the sport's governing body finds the will to act. But regrettably, the wind of change is so far a hardly discernable zephyr.

In 1986, to recall a prime example of Jockey Club immobility, the then recently retired jockey Edward Hide, a gifted and greatly experienced rider of the highest class, applied to become a stewards' secretary, one of the salaried staff who advise the amateur 'judges' on points of racing practice and law, rather in the manner of a magistrates' clerk.

Hide was rejected in favour of a former army officer and City gent with no practical experience of racing, a decision which left many professionals with a feeling of acute despair.

Rather than turning down men of Hide's merit and knowledge, racing should be seeking them out and offering worthwhile salaries for their much-needed services. Hopefully, whatever form a new Turf authority takes, one of its first changes will be to abolish this outmoded system and replace it by well-paid, well-respected professionals whose experience of race riding will mean an end to the current hit-and-miss disciplinary arrangement.

The problem of misbehaviour among race crowds may be less easily solved. Let me emphasise that the actions of the vast majority of the some four million annual racegoers in this country are exemplary and not, in any way, open to question.

But pockets of loutish and violent 'fans' are to be found on many of the country's 59 racecourses, particularly during the Soccer closed season. Drink has always been associated with racing but while it was once champagne in the summer and whisky to warm a winter's chill National Hunt afternoon, now the lager-swillers are all too much in evidence.

Graham Greene's razor gangs, to be found in the pages of that celebrated novel Brighton Rock, are, thankfully, no longer in evidence but swaying gangs of beered-up young rowdies, swearing at the tops of their voices and pushing their way around the enclosures are, it seems, now a fixture. At best their displays are unsavoury, at times dangerous and un-nerving. There are several racecourses where I would hesitate to take my wife on summer Saturday afternoons and where no child would be safe. Racing's long-standing image as a sport for family groups is being questioned in consequence and large sums of additional expenditure are being paid by racecourse managements to engage commercial security staff in order to counter the situation.

During a period of recession which has hit receipts in racing as all other leisure and sporting industries, this must be highly unwelcome. But leaders throughout the world have comprehensively failed to discover a solution to this modern malaise and, at least for the time being, it seems that we must live with the phenomenon occasioned by the unattractive side of youth culture.

Discipline within racing, now considered soft and ineffective by some traditionalists, was once unpleasant in the extreme. Stables were run on feudal lines with long hours, poor pay and physical punishments the norm. In some yards the life of stable lads was nothing short of bonded labour verging on downright slavery. Nor am I writing of a bygone age. Only during the last 20 to 30 years do we find conditions improving.

Apprentice jockeys fared hardly better than the lads and Joe Mercer, to become one England's greatest riders of the post-war era, can recall the harshness he found on becoming indentured to Major Frederick Blair Sneyd's stable at Sparsholt near Wantage in 1947.

'It was hard, very hard,' Mercer said. 'Major Sneyd was a tough man who expected his pound of flesh but I was properly taught, not just about stable routine and how to ride but the social graces as well. To start with I was put to menial tasks like weeding and stone picking, I even had to wait at table. And I got just two afternoons a week off, in other words I worked six long days and evenings out of seven. I would not like to start it all again.'

For all the effort Mercer was to receive, under the terms of his 12-year apprenticeship contract, the sum of three shillings a week for the first three years and 10 shillings a week for the remaining term. He was expected to ride free for his own stable but was paid two pounds, two shillings for a losing 'outside ride and three pounds, 13 shillings for a winner!

'Modern-day stable staff don't know how fortunate they are by comparison,' insists Mercer. 'But I was one of the lucky ones who made it all pay off in the end.'

For Mercer and other top-class jockeys financial rewards became large later in their careers. Now retaining fees and percentages have resulted in leading international stars frequently being richer than the owners for whom they ride. But the subservient past is still observed in one parade-ring gesture as millionaire jockeys touch their caps in respect to owners they could often afford to buy and sell. Present-day champion jockeys rate among the elite of sporting superstars with annual earnings in some cases beyond the six-figure barrier. Private aircraft, luxury cars and even country estates are well within their grasp.

No wonder they resent some old buffer in his capacity as a local steward informing them how to ride and perhaps imposing a ban which causes the loss of a Classic-race winner and many thousands of pounds in revenue! The fashionable and successful jockey is keen to ride more and more winners. He is not in the market to 'stop' a horse so that a big-betting owner or trainer may get longer odds next time. Nor is he willing to line a bookmaker's pockets. But lower down the earnings scale temptations are far greater.

A workaday rider just getting a living will find it much harder to resist a fat wad of 'readies' offered with minimum chance of getting caught. Although, in fairness to the brief of this publication, that hardly constitutes a decline in sporting behaviour. Given the nature of racing and betting it would be a totally naive notion to imagine that this was not always the case.

Saints are in short supply on the Turf and a certain pragmatism is usual. The trick is to keep cheating to a minimum and, conversely, integrity at a reasonable level. Britain's racing authorities have not always managed to bold that balance and still fall short of the ideal.

From time to time we see another, quite different, problem caused by competition becoming over-fierce. And this may well be on the increase. Disputes between jockeys rarely surface in the public eye but changing room battles are frequent enough and an exchange of blows now unknown.

Once again my source is Scobie Breasley who has been dining out for years on the subject of his Ascot clash with Lester Piggott in the 1960 King George VI and Queen Elizabeth Stakes.

The Australian master and his younger English rival always held each other's skills in suitable respect but it is fair to say they were never close friends and disinclined to help one another achieve a victory even in the most modest of races.

It was just such an event—at Wolverhampton—when Piggott, whose sense of humour is, to say the least, quirky, greatly upset Breasley by cutting across his mount and nearly putting him over the running rail. Breasley stormed into the weighing room intent on punching Piggott's nose but was held back by another jockey.

'He was right, of course,' Breasley admits now. 'It just wasn't worth risking my licence in a fit of temper and I decided instead to hit Lester where it would hurt him much more—in the wallet. I bided my time and the opportunity came on big-race day as Ascot when he was riding the brilliant filly Petite Etoile, considered unbeatable in the King George. My horse had no chance of winning but I decided to try and keep Lester from doing so and when he challenged on the inside in the home straight and was shouting for some room I just stayed right where I was.

'Petite Etoile couldn't get a run until it was too late and failed to catch the outsider Aggressor, ridden by Jimmy Lindley. I hadn't broken any rules, just been bloody-minded and although Lester knew what it was all about he never said a word and no stewards' enquiry was called. But he never cut me up again.

'Then, when all the Press boys wanted to know why Petite Etoile hadn't won as she was fully entitled to do, Lester came out with one of his best straight-faced comments by saying that they had mowed the grass the wrong way. Nobody knew what to make of that, he left them all with their mouths hanging open.'

I'm bound to say the secret saga of the 1960 King George is one of my favourite racing stories but Scobie Breasley was careful not to reveal it until after he had retired. Backers who laid the odds on the hot favourite that day more than 30 years ago might have found it less than funny. But in lengthy retrospect it seems an engaging tale although perhaps one that has improved in the telling with the facts blurred by the passage of years.

Lester Piggott's career, now gracefully and successfully resumed following his prison term for attempted tax fraud, is unique. He has partnered over 5,000 winners—more than any British jockey—but has had many clashes with racing authority over four decades. His fans, I am among the most devoted of them, will forgive Piggott almost anything because his talent is supreme. But stewards down the years have sometimes taken a less charitable view.

On another Ascot occasion he is reputed to have shouted 'move over grandad' at Sir Gordon Richards before barging his way through and earning a long suspension.

At Longchamp he 'borrowed' a leading French jockey's whip after dropping his own in a hectic big-race finish and told the enquiring stewards: 'Sorry, I thought he had finished with it.' They were not amused either and another ban was imposed.

But perhaps Greville Starkey was racing's biggest jockey. He perfected an impersonation of a Jack Russell Terrier and once used this 'gift' to telling effect during a race in South Africa.

'My horse was blocked by three others and I had no chance of getting a clear run,' he recalls. 'But when I did the Jack Russell act all the other jockeys looked round thinking there was a dog on the track and left a gap along the rails just wide enough for me to go through and win in a photo-finish. I think they're still looking for that dog to this day. They didn't know he caught the plane back to Heathrow a few hours later.'

Racing, once described by the late Phil Bull, founder of the Timeform organisation, as 'the world's greatest triviality,' is, in fact, a deadly serious business; the sporting world's biggest contributor to the Exchequer and, together with betting and Thoroughbred breeding, providing employment to more than 100,000 people in Britain alone.

It needs at least a facelift to continue prospering into the next century. But the basic requirement is new leadership to improve standards of discipline, integrity, performance and facilities.

The spoilsports must not gain a bigger foothold in what was once the Sport of Kings if it is to continue in the role of pastime for the people.

MOTOR RACING

David Smith

The admission was disarmingly frank and chilling. Yes, said Ayrton Senna, he had deliberately driven world championship rival Alain Prost off the track at the start of the 1990 Japanese Grand Prix.

Consider, just for a second, the implications of Senna's action. The sweeping right-hand corner which marks the end of the main straight at the Suzuka circuit is taken at over 150mph on a flying lap.

Even from a standing start the jostling cars are well into three-figure speeds before the drivers dab the brakes, select fourth gear and apply the slightest of turns to the steering wheel.

When two cars collide under such circumstances no-one, not the greatest driver nor the most well-informed engineer, can assume the inherent safety of those strapped tightly in what amounts to a four-wheeled missile containing 200 litres of highly flammable racing fuel.

Mercifully, Senna and Prost climbed from what remained of their cars without a scratch between them. Yet emotions still ran high that day in Japan. Prost, deprived of the chance to retain the title he had won under similar controversial circumstances at Suzuka twelve months earlier, was scathing in his criticism of Senna's tactics.

For his part, Senna vehemently denied any responsibility for the incident and travelled on to the final race of the year in Australia confirmed as the new world champion.

It so happened that the Adelaide Grand Prix was the 500th race to carry points counting towards the World Championship. To mark the occasion, a celebration photograph was taken on the starting grid. Former champions Sir Jack Brabham, Denny Hulme, Jackie Stewart, James Hunt and Nelson Piquet were among those who posed for the camera. But there, in the centre of the frame, was a smiling Senna, his right hand raising in salute the left arm of the legendary Juan-Manuel Fangio.

They sat in apparent harmony, bonded by a common love for speed, technical excellence and the acclaim that follows in the slipstream of triumph on the track.

Yet Fangio and Senna were also divided by an invisible chasm in the accepted standards of behaviour and attitudes both in the cockpit and away from the roaring melee.

It was not until a year after that black episode at Suzuka that Senna finally drew the curtain of pretence and revealed the malice behind his attack on Prost. It is a story of spite and suspicion which forms a bleak conclusion to this chapter on the decline in honour and integrity among those who drove, and continue to drive, around the circuits of the world.

There is a strong temptation to mourn the passing of those post-war races which formed the first World Championships. It was a time of honour amongst gladiators in their high-speed chariots who fought hard but fair with rivals they could also count on as friends.

But it was also a period of incredible wastage in terms of human life. Death quite literally lurked around every corner. That was not an irreverent cliche during the 1950s and 1960s, it was a stark reality.

In the ten years between 1980 and 1990 two drivers, Gilles Villeneuve and Ricardo Paletti, were killed during the course of a Grand Prix meeting. In the 20 dreadful years between 1953 and 1973, 17 drivers lost their lives during practice or in the race.

Among their number was Peter Collins, a dashing hero if ever there was one. Here was a fun-loving Englishman who won the hearts of the infamous *tifosi*—those Italian motor racing fans whose support for their national Ferrari team is fervent and intense in the extreme—over three decades before Nigel Mansell was to slip behind the wheel of one of the flame red cars from Maranello.

One episode involving Collins embodied the spirit of the time. Monza is the cauldron of Latin emotion that bubbles just outside of Milan. It was here that the 1956 World Championship was to be decided. Three men were chasing the title: Collins, Ferrari team-mate Fangio, and one Stirling Moss in a Maserati.

Fangio's challenge appeared doomed when his steering failed late in the race, but Collins sped into the pits and handed his machine over to the grateful Argentinian. Moss won the race but Fangio finished second to claim the fourth of his five World Championships.

Was Collins merely following team orders? Was he forced to enter the pits anyway to change a worn rear tyre? Or, as one report at the time would have it, did Collins believe in his own mind that he was not yet ready to shoulder the burden of pressure that goes with being World Champion?

We will never know for sure. What remains undisputed is the fact that Collins handed his car over to Fangio with good grace.

Two years later Collins was killed when his Ferrari clipped a bank and overturned at the old Nurburgring circuit while battling for the lead in the German Grand Prix with close friends Mike Hawthorn and Tony Brooks.

For them, the feuding which infests modern Grand Prix racing would have been an anathema, a view confirmed by Collins' widow Louise.

'I think the drivers respected each other too much for any of that stuff,' she said. 'There was etiquette, if you like, rules by which they played.

◄ Tamara Press was the epitome of the Eastern European woman athlete of the days gone by. She and her Soviet and East German compatriots dominated field athletics to an astonishing degree. At the time of this throw in 1966, her world record was 61ft.

▼ Irina and Tamara Press— champions at hurdles and shot respectively—are pictured in London in 1961. The drive to eliminate drug taking in athletics caused many athletes from several nations to "disappear" from the international scene very quickly.

◄ No sport has been more afflicted by drug abuse than athletics and no athlete so demeaned by being found guilty than Ben Johnson of Canada. Only hours after running the fastest 100 metres ever, at the Seoul Olympics, he was departing Korea in disgrace. Although eventually allowed to compete again Johnson has never repeated the remarkable times of 1988.

► Sugar Ray Robinson pictured in 1962, shortly before his fight with Terry Downes. It is claimed that Robinson was skilled in close quarter butting and that he regularly won fights by this spiteful tactic without ever being disciplined by the referee.

▲ Action by the non-combatants, the crowd and the corner men, has afflicted professional boxing in recent years with disputed decisions causing bottles to be thrown and scuffles to break out in the ring. Here, Delroy Ruddock has to be restrained after seeing his brother Donovan "Razor" Ruddock beaten by Mike Tyson.

► Nearly sixty years after the "bodyline" tour it is still debated whether this was an early example of bad sportsmanship, or of the legitimate use of tactics. Here, Jardine and Woodfull toss up for the Third Test Match at Adelaide.

◄ Jardine's firepower in
the "bodyline" tactic was
Harold Larwood, the
Nottinghamshire miner
whose pace and accuracy
made him an awsome
bowler on the fast
Australian wickets.

▼ A fiery personality can benefit a pace bowler required to retain his speed and hostility in game after game. Dennis Lillee, one of the finest of his speed, allowed occasional confrontations with the game's controllers to blight a brilliant career .

▼ Trevor Chappell, seen here with his Australian colleague, spinner Ray Blight, delivered the most controversial ball in the history of cricket when he rolled the ball underarm to prevent New Zealand scoring six off the last ball to tie a Test Match .

◄◄ The questioning of officialdom came later to cricket than many other sports. The "finger-wagging" incident between England's Mike Gatting and the Pakistani umpire Shakoor Rana had its origins earlier in the tour and, it might be argued, on earlier visits to the region.

► David Robertson remains the only professional golfer to be banned from the sport because of cheating. This former Scottish amateur international was caught during a qualifying round of the 1985 Open Championship.

◄ American golfer, Craig Stadler, was involved in a remarkable ruling in the 1987 San Diego Open when he took a towel from his golf bag to kneel on when faced with a tricky shot from beneath a bush. This apparently reasonable action to save a dry cleaning bill saw Stadler fall foul of the rule which does not allow the player to "build a stance".

► Arthur "Scobie" Breasley was one of the most successful of postwar flat-racing jockeys. He has long urged the ruling bodies of racing to allow former riders to take up course steward positions so as to bring an informed, experienced view to race control and disputes.

▼ Lester Piggott began his riding career forty-four years ago and has always courted controversy through his tough racing methods. His record of achievement will surely never be matched though he may well be remembered more than he would wish for his long prison sentence for tax offences. It has been the most remarkable feat of his sporting life to have come back to ride many winners after such a lay-off.

◄ Brazilian racing driver, Ayrton Senna, showed outstanding determination in the junior ranks of his sport even before he reached Formula One. Once in this spotlight his driving techniques and ruthlessness brought regular criticism from other drivers.

▼ Ayrton Senna would win the World Championship if Alain Prost failed to score points in the 1990 Japanese Grand Prix. Within 400 yards of the start and with Prost getting away faster, the two cars collided and skidded out of the race. Senna admitted, one year later, to causing the crash deliberately.

▲ Didier Pironi was
involved in a remarkable
dispute with Ferrari team-
mate Gilles Villeneuve at
the San Marino Grand Prix
of 1982 when he "stole" the
race from his colleague who
was slowing to conserve
fuel in the fond belief that
Pironi would obey pit
instructions and remain in
second place. Days later,
Villeneuve was killed in a
qualifying run; Pironi was
badly injured later in the
season and killed in a
powerboat race in 1987.

◄ The worst disciplinary
record in British
professional football is
probably held by Mark
Dennis whose career with
several clubs was blighted
by sendings-off and other
disputes. Dennis and
players like him will claim,
sometimes with
justification, that their
reputation precedes them
and causes officials to keep
a special watch on them.

▲ The "hand-of-God" goal which put Argentina in the lead against England in World Cup of 1986. The fact that Maradona claimed, and joyously celebrated, the "goal" did nothing for sporting etiquette but it was the disbelief of spectators and television viewers that the foul went unnoticed and unpunished by the referee and linesman at the time which was most marked.

► Graham Roberts (*bottom left*) and Terry Butcher, both England internationals but then playing for Glasgow Rangers, were two of the four players to appear before the Sheriff's Court in the city accused of disorderly conduct and committing a breach of the peace in Rangers—Celtic game in October 1987. This was the first instance of action being taken in the civil courts as a result of police reports of behaviour on a football pitch.

▼ The trials of the sports official! Most referees and umpires will confirm they are constantly subject to appeals, abuse and devious psychology as matches progress. They can never win and are regularly criticised when other adult temperaments boil over and they are left to adjudicate.

◄ Despite his controversial reputation and occasional disputes with the game's governing bodies, Brian Clough has always insisted on his players conducting themselves correctly both on and off the field. His playing staff are fully aware of the standards the manager has set and any which fail to meet them are disciplined by the Club.

▼ Though the high tackle in soccer is commonly penalised for the injury it can cause to the player being tackled, the 1991 FA Cup Final saw Paul Gascoigne come off worst in this celebrated incident. Gascoigne, who had starred in the World Cup, faced being sidelined with the subsequent injury for many months, so prejudicing his lucrative transfer to Italian club, Lazio.

► Like Nastase, Jimmy Connors has mellowed a little as his career has developed but these two fine players eroded the decorum which tennis had enjoyed from its inception. Now more noted for his "never-say-die" marathon games, Connors is seen here during such a game, against Michael Pernfors in 1987.

► Clown, showman or cheat? Ever ready to plead his cause with a smile on his face, Ilie Nastase brought a rebellious attitude to the court which had previously been absent from tennis.

▲ Uncontrollably confrontational, John McEnroe has at least been consistent! He has never accepted a close call when it has counted against him, and been ready to dispute the call when under close scrutiny by the media, as seen here. One wonders why no reporter has asked him if he really believes he has sole concession on disputed calls, and that his opponents do not suffer to an equal degree.

◄ Monica Seles can claim a good behaviour record on court but she has fallen foul of administrators by choosing to play lucrative exhibition matches instead of ranking tournaments.

► A gold medalist for Britain in two successive Commonwealth Games, Dean Willey lost his chance of a third medal when he was dropped from the 1990 squad after failing a routine drugs test. The competitor who won the gold for which Willey would have been favourite, Ricky Chaplin of Wales, was also found guilty of drug taking and was sent home without his title.

▼ The sophisticated and orderly ranks of show-jumping were rocked by video evidence that Paul Schockemohle, Germany's leading rider/trainer, used training methods deemed to be cruel by the television companies and sponsors which are so vital to the continuing success of the sport.

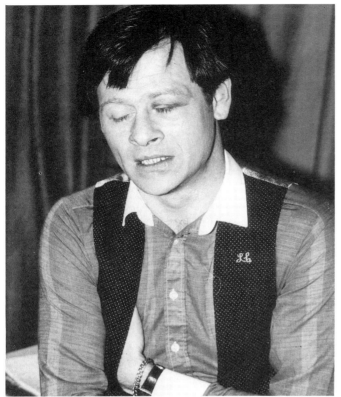

◄ There has never been any dispute about the playing ability of snooker's bad boy, Alex Higgins, but controversy has dogged his career with drink and drug accusations, criminal threats against other players and run-ins with officals making headlines rather than his playing performance. Here he sports a black eye as a result of being "kicked by a horse", an injury which intrigued TV viewers in 1986.

◄ Boris Onischenko, the Russian pentathlete, sits alone and disconsolate as he considers his disqualification from the Montreal event after it had been discovered that the recording device in his sword had been tampered with.

'Once in a while the boys would get angry with some young hotshot who thought he knew it all, and they'd talk to him about it. But they'd do it quietly, in private.

'In those days there was this feeling that they were doing something they loved and everyone was on the same side. There was certainly a feeling that racing was quite dangerous enough as it was, without people being crazy.'

Moss would undoubtedly concur with those sentiments. He was Fangio's team-mate at BRM and Mercedes before they raced against each other for the rival Italian Ferrari and Maserati outfits. 'That was an honourable period of motor racing,' he said, 'and regardless of whether we were team-mates or rivals I was fortunate to count Fangio as my friend, in many ways as a mentor, and always as the complete master of our sport.'

Team-mates, back in 1955, meant just that. It was at Aintree that year that Moss, driving a Mercedes, became the first home driver to win the British Grand Prix. But was he allowed to take the chequered flag by Fangio?

'I'd like to think that I won it fair and square,' said Moss, 'but I'm just not sure.'

Moss, admittedly with his foot flat on the accelerator, had waved the senior Mercedes driver by on the last corner of that race. But in front of a huge, cheering Merseyside crowd, Fangio kept formation and followed the young Englishman over the line.

Fangio, perhaps mindful of the public relations coup for Mercedes if Moss were to win the British round of the World Championship, told his team-mate: 'You were on form and that was your day.'

Much later, Moss was to recall: 'Fangio was such a gentleman. He was the sort of man to say: what the hell, I've won all the others.'

If such an attitude was so admirable then, what forces eroded it over the years to the point where a display of trust and generosity is the exception and not the rule at a Formula One Grand Prix?

To an extent, vastly increased safety standards have negated the need for chivalry between drivers. The spectre of death or injury still haunts the grid, but the reality is that the majority of drivers walk away from wrecked cars these days instead of being carried away on a stretcher.

Commercialism, too, has given the sport's image a sharper edge. When the cars began to resemble mobile billboards towards the end of the 1960s the cost of competing in Formula One, and the rewards on offer to those who were successful, began to rocket.

Entering the 1990s, top teams such as Williams and McLaren were operating on annual budgets approaching £30 million. And that figure does not take into account the huge investments made in racing engine technology by leading manufacturers such as Honda, Renault and Ford.

The drivers have not missed out on this new-found wealth either. Proven winners like Senna, Mansell and Prost could command annual retainers of up to £7 million. With such incentives on offer, it was hardly surprising that traditional values appeared to carry a price tag. Sportsmanship could be bought, sold and ultimately discarded.

Louise Collins considered her late husband's gesture to Fangio in the light of the modern game. 'Let's face it,' she said, 'in those days there wasn't the money so probably it was much easier to be a sportsman when you didn't have those kinds of colossal figures hanging over you.

'But in any case, Peter revered Fangio and he never felt there was much urgency about winning the World Championship. It always seemed to me he cared more about winning individual races.

'And he was very much a guy who cared about team spirit—if he hadn't enjoyed racing it wouldn't have been worth a damn to him.

'It was important, above all, that someone in a Ferrari won the World Championship. Probably, that doesn't make sense to anyone today.'

In 1982, it would have made sense to Gilles Villeneuve. He was the Best, the Ballesteros, the Muhammad Ali of motor racing: one of that rare breed of sportsmen whose mere presence in an arena sends a tingle of excitement and expectation racing down the spines of those privileged to be watching from the stalls or the terraces.

What made Villeneuve all the more remarkable was that, in a sport which had come to feed on ego and pretension, the little French-Canadian existed on an exclusive diet of fun and enthusiasm.

It is in this context that the circumstances behind his death during qualifying for the 1982 Belgian Grand Prix bear examination.

The story essentially started two weeks earlier in the San Marino Grand Prix at Imola. In qualifying, Villeneuve set a time nearly one and a half seconds faster than Ferrari team-mate Didier Pironi. Come the race, it was Villeneuve who harried the Renaults of Alain Prost and Rene Arnoux until the French cars retired, leaving him set to claim a first victory in front of his adoring Italian fans.

The one doubt in Villeneuve's mind was the ability of the Ferrari to go the distance without running out of petrol. Still, the only possible challenge could come from Pironi and Ferrari tradition dictated that the driver in the lead when the red cars took over first and second places was the driver who should take the chequered flag.

Thus, Villeneuve surmised, he could safely slow down to preserve fuel. He was surprised when Pironi took the lead in the closing stages and began lapping at racing speeds, but perhaps the Frenchman was just playing to the crowd?

Villeneuve regained the initiative and again attempted to put a brake on the worrying lap speeds. Again, however, Pironi raced past. By this time, even the Ferrari team management were expressing concern at the effect this duel was having on fuel consumption and hung messages out on the pit boards to warn their drivers.

Going into the last lap Villeneuve was back in front and confident that a cherished victory was his. But Pironi had other ideas. Almost within sight of home he whipped by to lead the two red cars over the line.

When Villeneuve returned to the pits and removed his crash helmet, disappointment and anger was etched across every sweaty inch of his face.

Jackie Stewart was among those at Imola that day. He reported: 'I had never seen Gilles angry like that . . . he was stunned. There had always been this innocence about Gilles. He didn't have a trace of maliciousness in him and he couldn't quite believe what had happened to him. It was awful that the last days of his life were so tormented and disillusioned.'

Later, Villeneuve was to open his heart to close friends and journalist Nigel Roebuck. 'Let me remind you of a bit of history,' he said. 'Remember Monza in 1979? I sat behind Jody Scheckter the whole way, knowing that this was my last chance to beat him for the World Championship.

'I hoped like hell that he would breakdown. But I never thought about breaking my word. I know all about team orders at Ferrari.

'Imola was going to be my race because I was in front of Pironi when Arnoux dropped out. If it had been the other way around then tough luck to me. I can tell you, and I know it to be true, that I would not have tried to take it away from Pironi, and I expected the same from him.

'Finishing second is one thing, I would have been mad at myself for not being quick enough if he'd beaten me. But finishing second because the bastard steals it . . . Jesus, that's why I'm mad.'

Villeneuve chose to disassociate himself from his team-mate, declaring: 'When we get to Belgium I'll race with him as if he had a Williams or a Brabham . . .'

Days later, during a qualifying run at Zolder, Villeneuve was flung to his death when his Ferrari hit the March of Jochen Mass and broke apart.

Alain Prost captured the sense of loss and frustration felt by those who had come into contact with Villeneuve.

He said: 'Gilles will always be remembered for his exceptional driving skills, his sincerity and his unbounded generosity. He was a very fine person, a living legend, and everyone in Formula One liked and respected him.'

For his part Pironi maintained that no team orders had existed at Imola and, whatever, he believed that Villeneuve's car was slowing because it had a mechanical problem. Those were the days, of course, before drivers had radio communications with the pits.

It is easy to take sides and cast aspersions in such cases. But consider the pressures on Pironi in 1982. Even before the start of the season he was being heavily backed as the first French winner of the World Championship. Two months into the campaign he survived a huge accident during testing at Paul Ricard; in April he got married; the same month saw the Imola controversy; in May Villeneuve was killed; in June Pironi stalled, through no fault of his own, on the grid in Canada and was rammed by newcomer

Ricardo Paletti who subsequently died of his injuries; there was another big crash at Ricard in which he sustained bruised legs.

Then, in August, with that historic championship within his grasp, Pironi's motor racing career was ended when he failed to spot Prost's car in blinding spray during a rain-soaked qualifying session in Germany. The Ferrari was launched into the air at 170mph. Pironi was lucky to survive the violent impact when his car crashed back to the track, but his legs sustained terrible injuries from which he never fully recovered. Pironi was killed five years later in a powerboat race.

Attempting to assess the inspirations and aspirations of the human mind is, by its very nature, a difficult science. In the case of the Imola controversy, we can only consider the two sides to the story and draw our own conclusions as to what drove Pironi and Villeneuve to take their respective courses of action.

There was another incident during the 1982 German Grand Prix, however, about which there can be no doubt because it was witnessed around the world by millions of stunned television viewers.

Bear in mind Louise Collins' insistence that hotshot newcomers to Grand Prix racing during the 1950s would be taken quietly to one side by their more experienced peers and have the facts of motor racing life spelled out to them in a dignified fashion.

Then consider Nelson Piquet's absurd resort to fisticuffs when his Brabham crashed out in a tangle with the ATS of relative novice Eliseo Salazar.

The circumstances leading to the crash remain open to argument. The two cars were approaching one of Hockenheim's notorious chicanes. Salazar, being lapped, ought to have given way. But then Piquet, the reigning world champion, knew he had a clear lead and might just as easily have backed off to tail the Chilean through the zig-zag and overtake him with comparatively little risk on the following straight.

In the event, neither man gave way. When the dust cleared and two stationary cars were picked out by the cameras, Piquet could be spied marching menacingly towards Salazar. The Brazilian suddenly led with a right hook and followed up with a left jab. This, don't forget, against an opponent wearing a crash helmet! Piquet must have realised the folly of this particular line of attack because he switched to Salazar's unprotected groin with his right boot.

Greg 'Peewee' Siddle was Piquet's friend and mentor. 'It's amazing how many people have seen that incident on TV and simply condemned Nelson,' said the Australian. 'But you have to get to know behind this story to understand the full implications.'

Siddle recounted the tale of how Piquet had driven away from a Formula Three meeting at Thruxton near Andover in 1979 and noticed a young man walking down the main road with a briefcase in his hand. It was not the best of weather, so Piquet offered the stranger a lift. His grateful passenger turned out to be Salazar, who had just arrived in Britain with virtually nothing but a briefcase full of money with which to buy himself into a Formula Three team. Piquet passed the newcomer on to Siddle, who was able to help establish him in single seater racing.

'What irked Nelson at Hockenheim,' said Siddle, 'was that Salazar, the guy he literally picked up at the side of the road, was totally to blame. Nelson told me his first reaction had been to head-butt him in the chest. But he decided not to do that because he realised it might break his ribs. So then he vented his anger in the way that the world saw in such detail.'

An explanation maybe, but hardly an excuse that would have found a sympathetic ear with Peter Collins. Indeed, one can only speculate on how long Piquet would have lasted in an era when rivals on the track swapped pints and not punches off it.

One standard had, until 1988, never been challenged. As British racing driver Derek Warwick explained: 'Families are off limits.'

Piquet tore up that convention when he gave an interview to Playboy magazine in his native Brazil. Piquet, it should not be forgotten, had by now won the World Championship three times. Only Fangio had scored more titles. Yet, while one South American wore the crown with dignity, the other tarnished it with unwarranted personal attacks upon those connected with the sport including Senna, Mansell and, in particular, Mansell's wife Rosanne.

The British driver, Piquet's former team-mate at Williams, remained commendably aloof from any physical confrontation. 'Piquet is just a vile man,' he said. 'But then I was already aware of that.'

Ironically, Mansell and Senna, rapidly gaining a reputation for a supremely confident style of driving bordering on the intimidatory, had themselves clashed one year earlier at the 1987 Belgian Grand Prix. Their cars had spun in perfect unison while battling for the lead, Senna's Lotus becoming stuck in a sand trap while Mansell later retired his Williams with bodywork damage.

It was inevitable that each man should blame the other for the incident. Mansell, however, let his emotions get the better of him and he marched down the pit lane to confront Senna in the Lotus garage.

'I knew he hadn't come to apologise because his face wasn't right for that and you are not apologising when you get hold of someone by the throat,' shrugged Senna.

Mansell replied: 'I am not, for one minute, condoning what I did. But someone had to do something to that guy and subsequently, coincidence or not, I haven't had one bit of trouble with him. If anything, he's become almost the perfect gentlemen. I think I made my point so forcibly that he'll think twice about doing anything silly with me again.'

Senna would win his first World Championship for McLaren in 1988. His hopes of retaining the title the following year hinged on him winning the penultimate race at Suzuka in order to close the points gap on McLaren team-mate Prost.

For 46 laps, Prost kept Senna at bay. On the 47th lap, Senna made a lunge for the lead at the chicane. Did he expect Prost to make room? Did Prost not see the red and white car spearing down the inside? Whatever, they touched. Prost retired on the spot. Senna got going again with the aid of a bump start and went on to take the chequered flag. But he never received the nine precious points that went with it. The race stewards decided his action in regaining the track by going through the chicane and not around it was illegal, and Senna was disqualified. With that part went his hopes of beating Prost to the title.

The row over who caused the collision rumbled on for months, with Senna expressing particular concern over the part played by Jean-Marie Balestre, the autocratic French president of motor sport's governing body FISA (Federation Internationale du Sport Automobile).

Yet that kerfuffle was as nothing compared to the collision at a rather higher speed at Suzuka the following year, again involving Senna and Prost.

This time Prost, now driving for Ferrari, needed the win to stay in touch with Senna in the championship chase. A tense atmosphere was strained even further when there was confusion over which side of the track Senna, fastest in practice, should start. Again Balestre was involved in the row and the upshot saw Prost place his car on the cleanest piece of tarmac.

Sure enough, Prost made the better start and was ahead turning into the first corner. That was as far as he got. Senna held the tighter line into the right hander and ran into the Ferrari's rear wheel. In an instant both cars were careering into the gravel trap. Piquet won the race, but Senna was champion for a second time.

Prost was livid. 'If everybody wants to drive in this way, then the sport is finished,' he raged. 'Senna is completely opposite in character to what he wants people to believe. He is the opposite of honest. Motor racing is sport, not war . . . we were not even side by side. If Senna's behaviour is to be expected, then we will perhaps get to a situation where people will start entering a team with one car specifically intended to push off the opposition to enable the other guy to win.'

Senna's response was emphatic. It was, he insisted, a legitimate overtaking manoeuvre. The accident was Prost's fault, not his. 'I was coming faster than him,' said Senna, 'because I had more acceleration. I think Prost made a big mistake to close the door on me in the first corner.'

Opinions in the paddock were divided. Most, it appeared, sided with Prost. But others, including some eminent names in motor sport, were swayed by Senna's argument. Just as at Imola nine years earlier, the matter would have remained open for debate.

Then, on the occasion of clinching his third World Championship at Suzuka in 1991, the enigmatic Senna made his startling admission: he had meant to crash into Prost.

Without a trace of contrition he looked into the television cameras and put his case in slightly faltering but well-measured English. 'In '89 was a disgraceful end (to the championship) when I won the race . . . and it was taken away from me. I was prevented from going to the podium by Balestre and I never forgot that.

'The result of that was the 1990 championship when we fought all the way, myself and Prost, and we came to the last race and pole position was set in the wrong place. We agreed before the start of qualifying that pole position would be on the outside, then Balestre gave the order after qualifying not to change and I found myself on the wrong side of the track.

'I was so frustrated that I promised myself that if, after the start, I lose the first place, I would go for it in the first corner. Regardless of the result. I would go for it and Prost wouldn't turn into the first corner ahead of me. And that is what took place. And that was the result of the politicians making stupid decisions, and bad decisions.'

In a nutshell, Senna deliberately crashed into another car out of spite.

Journalist Denis Jenkinson, revered throughout motor racing for his unrivalled experience and perceptive observations of the Grand Prix scene, wrote of Fangio: 'It was an honour to know this remarkable man, who still carries with him that uncanny air of 'World Champion' wherever he appears. Young drivers of today still feel deep emotion when they meet the Grand Old Man of Grand Prix racing. The name itself is enough: Fangio—a true master of the art of Grand Prix racing and one who is respected the world over.'

Different eras breed different kinds of men. How, one wonders, will Senna be remembered? With admiration for a supreme driving talent? Without question. But with respect and honour? Somehow, I doubt it.

RUGBY UNION

Chris Jones

Rugby Union is a sport that requires exceptional self discipline. By its nature the game involves full body contact and there is always the opportunity to step over the line between total commitment and unacceptable violence. The sport is attaining a higher profile every year and the effect is to bring each highly visible outbreak of foul play into the living rooms of a public that immediately believes the sport is spiralling out of control.

The truth is very different. The number of sending offs in English rugby, by the far the largest rugby union in the World, has remained around the 1600 mark since the early 1980's and shows no immediate signs of leaping forward. The number of sending offs are small when you consider that around 300,000, (taking the lowest accepted figure) play the sport in England 36 Saturdays every year. But, there is tangible evidence within that figure of 1600 to suggest a decline in behaviour which *is* extremely worrying. Punching has been the favourite way of sorting matters out on the rugby pitch since the game was codified in the last century. If you were spotted swinging a punch it warranted either a severe warning or early bath. Now, the rules of the violence game are changing and the punch has been joined by the head butt and boot in the roll of dishonour.

It is the rise of the two new methods of violence in the field that is worrying players, coaches, referees and administrators across the World.

David Spyer, a former London Society referee, is still closely involved in the Society and compiles the Rugby Football Union's figures for dismissals from the field of play. His painstaking efforts provide the crucial insight into the spread of the boot and head butt at a time when coaches and selectors are being ordered not to select players with a history of violence. Spyer said; 'Kicking an opponent on the ground was unheard of in the early 1970's when I was refereeing top class rugby. There were, in the middle of the 70's, 232 players sent off for this offence in a total of 615 for violent play.

'Now, the proportion is very different. In 1990-91 there were 478 dismissed for using the boot or head butt from a total of 848. It was a very worrying situation and, I say again, that I would not have received a single report from a referee following a sending off, that dealt with kicking or head butting 'in the 70's.'

However, for many, the most sickening example of uncontrolled violence came at the start of the 1975 second test between Australia and England in Brisbane. The images of that disgraceful incident remain in the memory of anyone who sits through the television evidence. At the time it was so violent ordinary rugby supporters could not believe that an international team like Australia could have devised a plan to kick and punch the opposition with vicious brutality right from the start. It was a shameful attempt to dominate and it only succeeded in bringing the game in disrepute. Amazingly no Australian was sent off. The only man to be dismissed was England prop Mike Burton for a late tackle minutes after the ugly brawl had been stopped.

I remember sitting amongst a room full of people in Cardiff in 1981 waiting for the start of a film designed to highlight a growing problem in rugby. Without introduction the film started and that 1975 test match flashed onto the screen. The room fell silent as the pictures told the story without commentary. The most 'striking' incident involved an Australian forward repeatedly kicking the face of an England player who had been knocked to the ground. The film ended and still there was silence. Eventually the chairman of the discussion spoke and it was like a mass application of smelling salts. People all around me came to life and the noise level increased. Some were nervously laughing while others expressed, as everyone does on seeing the film, absolute horror that it could have happened on a rugby pitch.

The audience was made up of referees from all over the rugby playing world who had come to Cardiff for a special congress. It was part of the Welsh Rugby Union's centenary celebrations and that film helped focus everyone onto the subject of violence in the game.

It is referees who have to order the lunatics off and, with the increasing television and media interest, they have a terribly difficult task to perform. Without the ref you cannot play the game and, unlike association football, the man with the whistle does not have to suffer constant bad mouthing from the players. He has the power to march the loose-lipped back an extra ten yards each time they disagree with a decision. Take that respect away and it is a recipe for mayhem. With the game now boasting leagues in England that involve more than 1,700 clubs, the pressure is increased on players and officials. Mistakes really do have a telling effect, and unfortunately, there is evidence that referees are taking more stick than ever.

Thankfully, it has not reached the situation prevalent in soccer but the trend is there and is having an effect on recruitment. The London Society loses 50 referees a year through retirements or resignations. It is a constant battle to top up the pool which is needed to control matches from representative level down to colts. With the increased interest in rugby comes large crowds made up of people who are not in possession of a law book. Everyone has their say when a decision is made but the abuse now being hurled at referees from the touchlines is attaining an unprecedent volume. 'We are very perturbed by the unacceptable level of abuse from spectators;' said Spyer.

'The public are largely ignorant about the laws and when referees act as touch judges in league and cup matches they are subjected to intolerable verbal abuse. Clubs are now putting into programmes an explanation of just what a touch judge is allowed to signal for and they are no longer identifying which county the touch judge comes from. This is because they are abused if their home county happens to coincide with one of the teams playing in the game.

'It is all making it increasingly difficult to attract new referees to replace those who are leaving.'

If clubs cannot control the abuse from paying customers what can they do about the degenerating behaviour on the pitch? Referees have won backing from the RFU in their attempts to make clubs isolate the thugs. Known hit men are still being picked despite attempts to push them out of the sport. It is still a fact that players all over England are appearing before county disciplinary committees for the seventh or eighth times in their careers. Life bans are handed out very rarely and some county committees are, for reasons that are unclear, not invoking the RFU automatic 60 day bans for the worst kinds of violence. Inconsistency is rife in selection, refereeing and sentencing which only helps undermine the battle to beat the violent minority.

One argument put forward by those who wield a feather duster instead of a big stick at the hit men, is that they are only following the leniant lead given by international rugby players and officials. The game at the top also has its idiots and national selectors are just as slow to weed them out. France has always mixed magical running with a vicious forward effort and club rugby in that country is much 'dirtier' than in other parts of the rugby playing world. It is no surprise that this permeates into the Test arena. The effect is to put onto the television screen an unacceptable version of what is allowable in the game of rugby union. Youngsters imitate their heroes but when the people they look up to are like the Begles front row then the game is in real trouble.

The Begles front row came to the fore in 1990-91 when their club won the French championship fuelled by a formidable forward effort. The shaven headed front row of Simon, Gimbert and Moscato scare the hardest of rugby men. As a unit they are fearsome and, tragically for the game, they take the macho bit too far.

In successive internationals against Romania and the USA in 1991 this front row trip helped kick two players off the pitch. Ion, the Romanian hooker, departed from the field in Bucharest with blood streaming from his head and covering the yellow jersey he wore. After the match he said; 'You play for nearly two months in New Zealand against the hardest most competent rugby men in the World. They are tough and don't take prisoners. But, they are fair—they don't play dirty. They don't niggle you, pull your jersey, kick you in the head when you are down. In other words, you play rugby and don't have to worry about anything else.

'With the French it is different. They pull your jersey, they punch you from the first scrum, they spit and try to disrupt you as much as possible. After our first exchange when I was punched in the opening scrum and we started fighting they obviously targeted me. I was caught in the bottom of a ruck when I saw the boot coming down on my head. I have no doubt it was deliberate. They could have blinded me. I had five stitches in my eyelid and nine in the ear.'

Across the Atlantic the French trio were at it again in a country where rugby union is trying to attract young players in a sporting forum where American Football is King. The front row of France targeted American hooker Tony Flay in the first of two test matches. Flay found himself, like Ion, stuck at the bottom of a ruck and Simon stamped on his head twice. Flay had to be replaced by Pat Johnson whose nose was broken by a punch at a scrum. Simon went on to start fights with the American No8, spat in the face of his opposite number and purposely aimed himself at American players binding on the sides of rucks and mauls. This was designed to cause damage to unprotected ribs. Simon managed to break one American's ribs and spring the rib cartilage of another. The second test saw the French change their front row and bring back those who had seen service before the Begles trio hit the headlines. At the first scrum of that second test, Ondarts, a hard and experienced French prop, looked at his opposite number and said: 'no punching today'. There wasn't.

England's 1991 summer tour to Australia was marred by a deliberate stamping act by Geoff Didier, an Australian representative player. He twice trod on Simon Halliday's face as the England player tried to get away from a ruck. Like the incidents involving the French, the referee did not send the offender off. Didier was just warned and, by his inaction, the referee gave a clear signal to the youngsters watching that you can kick someone in the head and not be sent off. The referee thus became as guilty as the player who committed the foul act.

It takes courage to send an international rugby player off. There are 50,000 fans in the stadium, millions watching on television including fellow referees and assessors. But, if the men with the whistle in these games shirk their responsibility what hope is there for refs down the line who face similar dilemmas.

If the World of rugby was perfect then clubs would ban dirty players, coaches would refuse to allow them on the pitch, captains would turn their backs and play with only fair minded players, and referees could forget about the laws concerning foul play. As the real World is nothing like that, the opportunity for the violent to survive is always there. But, where do they come from, these unwanted players who believe a result is something created by a swinging punch or boot? You don't suddenly learn to be indisciplined after years of fair play.

The seeds of violence are sown in the schools and colts rugby systems and, if allowed to take root, they grow into a variety of rugby player epitomised by the Begles Boys.

Two of the last three youth matches I played in Wales ended early with the referee deciding he had to abandon the match. Violence, repeated incidents not single outbreaks, was the reason each time for the abandonment. The referees were local club officials who volunteered to help out. They were not qualified to referee but without their presence the matches could not have been played. Both games were ended with barely ten minutes remaining and this is a pattern that is seen in the figures produced by David Spyer.

My games were called off because the referee never really had control and lost the respect of the players. One side was losing by a healthy margin and frustration boiled over into personal battles that quickly engulfed both packs. Colts rugby is a real worry for all involved in policing the sport because the scenario I was involved in twice, is still repeated all too frequently in English rugby every season. Spyer explained; 'Ten years ago we made a conscious decision in the London Society to improve the standard of referees being assigned to Colts rugby matches. But, sadly there are still too many matches being abandoned because of violent play and referees are reporting verbal abuse and a lot of ignorant behaviour.

Spyer continued 'It is a problem we are trying to solve but the evidence shows that bad language is rife amongst the players, managers and coaches at the level and it is all very worrying.'

Dick Best, coach to England, London and Harlequins, has a reputation as a hard coach who produces attractive running rugby teams. He has a simply explained attitude to the rugby thug; 'If I see one of my players stamping on a head then that's the last time he ever steps onto a pitch for a team I coach. There is no place in the game for someone like that at any level, be it Colts or international standard.

'I believe that clubs, at all levels, are aware of the problems created by picking regular offenders and hopefully strong action will help curb these incidents.

'There is a big problem concerning the refereeing of certain aspects of play. In the Southern Hemisphere the attitude is that if you are stopping the ball coming out then the opposition can ruck you out with their boots. Rucking is very different to stamping. The leg moves at a different angle— backwards not up and down. In Britain the coaching of rucking is not good and young players go into those contact situations with poor technique and stamping results. Ignorance is a problem along with interpretation. If the referee is consistent and lets the players know what is allowed then incidents can be avoided.'

With rugby clubs upgrading their facilities and improving their coaching panels there is the possibility for a better future. Referees are more aware of the requirements of their position. Too many have been found wanting in the final quarter of matches when fitness is called into question. Up to 70 per cent of all sending offs occur in the final quarter when fatigue amongst players and the referee lead to mistakes and loss of discipline.

Improved fitness all round aligned to a commitment to eject the indisciplined players from the game will have a real effect on rugby. Unless all those involved in the sport commit themselves to this end, moves to change the face of rugby will gain increased backing from groups worried by the violence and resultant injuries. The Southern Hemisphee countries want to de-power the scrums and take action to negate areas of potential conflict. Parents do not want their children hurt and that concern for safety should continue until a player finishes his career in the Old Rugbymadaboutthegame Vets XV.

Rule changes alone will never be the answer if those who epitomise the decline in behaviour on the rugby pitch are selected week after week by clubs prepared to risk finishing with 14 men in a bid to get a win.

'Hopefully, we can hold the line at its present level and the thugs will be weeded out;' concluded Spyer.

SOCCER

Michael Hart

Little more than a century ago soccer remained a brutal form of recreation, a disorganised, lawless pastime initially pursued most vigorously by the working classes before creeping into the schools, colleges and universities.

It was among the country's academics and intellectuals that the rules which the world now accepts as The Laws of the Game were originally devised. But even they were divided on which route Association Football should follow.

Lord Kinnaird, later to become Lord High Commissioner for the Church of Scotland, was one of the sports great characters and enthusiasts. A fearless half back who sported a huge, bushy beard and wore long white flannels and a blue and white quartered cricket cap on the field of play, he cared little for the growing feeling within the game at the time that deliberate shin-kicking should be outlawed.

Before a match between his Old Etonians team and the Old Harrovians, led by Charles Alcock, later to become secretary of the Football Association, Kinnaird scoffed at Alcock's question: 'I say Arthur shall we play fair or shall we have hacking?'

Kinnaird replied: 'Oh! Let's have hacking!'

Hacking was deliberate shin-kicking, for centuries an accepted part of a game where skill traditionally took second place to vigour, if not violence.

Football, as it is played throughout the world today, began in England in the mid-19th century but there is evidence that a form of the game was played in China before the birth of Christ, and by the Greeks, the Romans and ancient Mexican Aztecs. Legend has it that the first game played among the Anglo-Saxons was a victory celebration using the severed head of a defeated Dane as a ball.

The early forerunner of the modern game in England was a timeless brawl between neighbouring parishes. It was when these roistering crowds began to spill aggressively through the streets of towns and villages that royal disapproval was first shown.

In 1314 Edward II proclaimed: 'Forasmuch as there is a great noise in the city caused by hustling over large balls, from which many evils may arise, which God forbid, we command and forbid, on behalf of the King, on pain of imprisonment, such game to be used in the city in the future.'

Neither that ban, nor future edicts of Edward III (1349), Richard II (1389), Henry IV (1401) stopped the playing of football. In Tudor England football was a savage game played without rules, except the unwritten ones of local custom. The Puritans furiously condemned 'the bloody and murthering practice.'

In the 16th century the English pamphleteer Philip Stubbes, in his An Anatomie of Abuses, wrote that football caused 'fighting, brawling, contention, quarrel-picking, murder and great effusions of blood, as daily experience teacheth.'

Sir Walter Scott championed football in Scotland and not only provided financial backing for his team, Men of Selkirk, but wrote ballads about them too. He also wrote, in 1815, that 'it was not always safe to have even the game of football between villages; the old clannish spirit is too apt to break out.'

For some reason, Shrove Tuesday became the day of the greatest blood-letting in the football calendar—sometimes as many as 500 a side kicking off in market places all over the country. At sunset the survivors were still playing. The modern football term 'derby match' comes from the annual encounter between the rival parishes of St. Peters and All Saints in the town of Derby. The last recorded contest in that town was on Shrove Tuesday 1846.

Two years later an attempt was made at Cambridge University by 14 men representing public schools like Eton, Harrow, Winchester and Rugby to draw up a set of common laws for the game but it wasn't until the formation of the Football Association in London in October 1863 that holding, tripping or hacking an opponent running with the ball was finally outlawed.

The formation of the FA was a bitter affair caused chiefly by the stubbornness of those supporting the Rugby code and those supporting the dribbling code. The split eventually became too wide ever to be mended. The argument was over hacking. The Rugby men felt it was manly and therefore acceptable to tackle an opponent by kicking him on the shin. The dribbling men did not, and voted it out. The Rugby men called the dribbling men cowards and walked out of the FA for ever.

Alcock was one of the FA men responsible for the 13 laws that provide the foundation for the modern game. Lord Kinnaird, and his supporters, reluctantly accepted the demise of 'hacking'. He, in fact, went onto play in a record nine FA Cup Finals.

The introduction of an organisational framework for the game—by the FA and the Football League, which was formed, the first of its kind in the world, in 1888—generated new challenges and new pressures. Professionalism was already a fact of life in football but rewards for the players were small and competition was generated mostly by local prestige.

Now, of course, there were reputations to be made at a national and international level. The first England-Scotland match was played in 1870. The behaviour of players on the field was influenced by intensifying competition, poorly defined rules, indifferent referees and growing crowds of spectators.

Scottish full back Alec Dick of Everton became the first footballer to be cautioned by the League for his behaviour on the field after allegations that he had struck a Notts County player and used foul language. After discussing his case the League proposed that Dick 'be requested to apologise for the ungentlemanly language he used on the Notts ground.' But they found the charge of striking an opponent not proven.

Significantly the infant League requested County not to report the case to their parent body, The Football Association. At that time the League obviously wanted to keep its dirty linen well hidden.

Then, as now, discipline within the sport was primarily the responsibility of the game's lawmakers, the FA. Complaints about rough play were heard so often that Tom Charnley, the secretary of the Football League, from 1902-33, sent a circular to all referees in 1910.

It read: 'Dear Sir, Reports are continually being received that the many unfair and unscrupulous tactics indulged in by some of the players in League football are allowed to pass unpunished by referees. In other instances the punishment is inadequate.

'The Management Committee are of the opinion that referees are not exercising full powers as required by the laws of the game and desire to further point out that they are remiss in their duties as referees in not taking cognisance of these offences, which they should penalise as to have a salutary effect on the offenders.

'Rough and dangerous play, likely to injure players, should be at once stopped, discrimination being made between 'robust' and 'rough' play. Firmness should be used at the start of the game and little trouble, generally, will be afterwards experienced.

'The Management Committee not only ask, but expect, referees to at once penalise actions which are calculated to injure the general character of the games.'

Five years later, with Britain in the midst of the Great War, the League still operating and the public increasingly hostile to professional footballers, two incidents occurred that brought disgrace and discredit to both the players and the game.

During a bad tempered match between Middlesbrough and the First Division leaders Oldham, played in pouring rain before 7,000 spectators in April 1915, the Oldham players foolishly kicked the ball away from the centre spot when the referee tried to re-start the game after Middlesbrough had scored a goal. Then, in the 56th minute, with Middlesbrough leading 4-1, the referee sent off the Oldham right back William Cook for a foul. Cook refused to leave the pitch, leaving the referee H. Smith, of Nottingham, no choice but to abandon the game.

It was a quite unprecedented incident in the history of the Football League. The Management Committee wanted to ban Cook permanently but the FA, instead, suspended him for one year.

That same Easter weekend relegation—threatened Manchester United were playing Liverpool at Old Trafford. United won 2-0 but the result had been pre-arranged by a handful of players—a fact that was patently obvious to most of the 15,000 spectators.

Faced with the prospect of no summer wages and a call up to go to the front, eight players clubbed together to make a quick killing with a betting coup. At the time it was possible to bet on a single result and so the conspirators had backed United to win 2-0.

The Football League's commission of enquiry, supported by conclusive evidence from the bookmakers, reached a verdict in December 1915 and banned the eight players from football sine die.

This, then, was part of the legacy the early professionals left to the modern game. Less easy to catalogue and evaluate is the basic competitive instinct of man.

Football, by its very nature, is a physical contact sport and has always appealed to the aggressive character of man. But the social climate has changed over the centuries and, ultimately, organisations like the Football Association and the Football League provided a lawful framework for a competitive, contact sport.

The fact that football flourished and became the most popular sport in the world suggests that a changing society found it an acceptable past-time.

But the professional players of the modern game now face pressures that were undreamed of a century ago. These pressures have built slowly over the years but the essential elements of the Laws of the Game have experienced little change.

The gentlemen amateur, if such ever existed, has gone. Competition in the modern professional game is intense. The pressure from coaches and managers, fearful of losing, is unrelenting. The expectation of supporters is high. The financial rewards for players and clubs can be immense. National pride can also generate emotions out of all proportion to the mere playing of a football match. El Salvador's bitterly disputed elimination of their Central American neighbour Honduras in 1969 in the World Cup qualifying programme provoked a short and bloody war between the two countries.

Add to these pressures the all-seeing eye of television and the media and we begin to get beneath the veneer of professional football and understand what motivates and influences the great players of the modern game. Which of these elements prompted Diego Maradona, acknowledged as the world superstar of the eighties, to commit the most heinous act of cheating in the 1986 World Cup finals in Mexico?

When the captain of Argentina deliberately punched the ball past England goalkeeper Peter Shilton in the quarter finals practically everyone in the 114,500 crowd in the Aztec Stadium in Mexico City suspected that he had touched the ball with his hand. Maradona knew he had. Shilton, who protested vehemently to the referee, knew he had. Television film proved it conclusively. Yet neither the referee nor his linesmen saw the incident.

Maradona later claimed that the goal was scored by 'the Hand of God.' Why did he, the idol of so many youngsters around the world, cheat in this way?

Was it for personal pride? National prestige? Financial gain? Was it because of the pressures placed on him by the Argentine management? Was it because of the expectation of the Argentine press and public? Was it his response to the tackling he had weathered from the England defenders? Was is simply instinctive?

Or was he merely reflecting the modern social climate: bending the rules, testing the strength of authority to see what he could get away with?

Few players with publicly admit to cheating. Equally, few will go throughout their playing career without cheating to some degree at some time. The cynics would argue that Maradona's only sin was that he was found out.

Handling the ball by an outfield player in football is not a common offence because it is too easily spotted by referees and opponents. Handling the ball was originally an essential part of the sport but the introduction of the FA's Laws of the Game confined handling the ball to goalkeepers.

The institution of the laws, the greater diligence of referees and the growing severity of punishments did, of course, influence the behaviour of players on the field. There is no doubt that football, as it is played today, is significantly less violent and more law-abiding that it was 200 years ago.

But, the pressures to win are greater than they were then and, human nature being what it is, many players presented with the opportunity to sneak an unseen advantage that breaks the laws, will do so.

Not all misbehaviour, of course, is premeditated. Frequently, desperation, recklessness or anger provoke a player to flout the rules. Perhaps most common in the high-speed tensions of the modern game is the dangerous tackle. It is not always meant to be dangerous, but is can inflict serious injury on the victim and, occasionally, the perpetrator.

Paul Gascoigne, the talented but unpredictable Tottenham and England midfield player, jeopardised a lucrative £5.5 million transfer to Lazio in Italy with an appaling foul on Gary Charles, of Nottingham Forest, in the 1991 FA Cup Final at Wembley. The felled Charles eventually struggled back to his feet, but Gasciogne was stretchered off the field and taken to hospital where he underwent a serious knee operation that threatened his imminent move to Italy and, in fact, his entire career.

From its earliest days football in Britain has been physically competitive and the modern game has inherited those qualities of endurance and ruggedness. The British player, therefore, has been traditionally admired and envied on foreign fields for courage, athleticism, resolute commitment and a sense of honour.

The British player today remains among the most competitive in the world, though the reputation for fair play has diminished. 'A part of the attraction of the English First Division, and British football in general, is the competitiveness and I don't think we should ever take that out of the game,' said the Liverpool manager Graeme Souness.

An intimidating and ruthless midfield player with Liverpool and Scotland, Souness epitomised the formidable resolve of the top British professional. His tackling and his ability to dominate opponents were among the reasons why Sampdoria of Italy signed him from Liverpool.

Football among the Latin nations evolved alongside the British game but tended to reflect the temperamental and emotional characteristics of the Latin races. They may have lacked some of the British tenacity, but they compensated with grace and skill and they, too, learned subtleties that infringed the Laws of the Game.

Some of the most tempestuous confrontations in the history of football have been between British and Latin teams. One of the most notorious was in 1967 in the World Club Championship Cup, an unofficial and troublesome trophy inaugurated to determine the world's top club by pairing the winners of the European Cup with the winners of the South American Cup.

As European champions, Celtic qualified to meet Racing Club of Argentina, the champions of South America. The teams played the first leg at Hampden Park, Glasgow, in October 1967, not much more than a year after the Argentine captain Antonio Rattin had been controversially sent off against England in the World Cup at Wembley. Alf Ramsey, the England manager at the time, fuelled the ill-feeling by denouncing the talented but fiery Argentine side as 'animals,' evoking almost paranoid reactions from the River Plate.

In the early stages of that World Cup the Argentines were censured by FIFA, the world governing body, for 'unethical tackling'. In the match against England, the tiny, bald-headed German referee Herr Kreitlin, inscribing names in his notebook with a schoolboy zeal, was the subject of a constant stream of verbal abuse and harassment from Rattin who was cautioned, before his sending off, for a foul on Bobby Charlton. That the Scots regarded England as their bitterest footballing foe was either not known or conveniently forgotten when Racing Club faced Celtic at Hampden Park. The animosity was apparent from the very first seconds of the match. The players of Racing Club employed an alarming array of professional fouls including body checking, shirt pulling, spitting and punching. It was premeditated intimidation designed to test the Celtic temperament.

The Scots had few answers to such sly gamemanship but retained their composure long enough to score a single goal. In the circumstances it was a slender lead to take to Argentina. Bob Kelly, the Celtic chairman, had seen enough in the first match to realise what lay in store for Celtic. He urged Jock Stein to boycott the return match, but his proud manager would not hear of such a suggestion. It was the biggest mistake of his illustrious career.

A hostile crowd set the tone for the second leg. Before the kick off the Celtic goalkeeper Ronnie Simpson was struck by a bottle thrown from the crowd and ruled out of the game. But Stein's faith in the tolerance level of his players seemed to be justified early in the first half when the volatile Jimmy Johnstone swept into the penalty area only to be sent crashing by a rugby tackle. Celtic scored from the penalty spot but, in the second half, conceded two goals and the match ended with the aggregate score 2-2.

On reflection it would have been wiser to share the Championship trophy, but Stein agreed to play a deciding game on a neutral ground in Montevideo, Uruguay three days later. Racing were as aggressive and provocative as ever in the third game. The little winger, Johnstone, who had to wash spittle from his hair at the end of the second match, elbowed an opponent in the face and was quite rightly sent off. The Celtic frustration simply boiled over. In the second half Bobby Lennox and John Hughes were also sent off and, late in an ugly match, Tommy Gemmell received his marching orders, but remained on the field apparently unaware of the full extent of the referee's displeasure.

There was no excuse for the behaviour of the Celtic players. But it was clear that Racing's cynical manipulation of controlled aggression had secured for them the Club Championship of the World.

Celtic were reprimanded, the players fined and the good name of British sportsmanship ridiculed. Stein was forced to apologise on behalf of his shamed team.

At the heart of this farcical series of confrontations lay the diverse footballing philosophies of two nations and the inability of referees to interpret the Laws of the Game consistently. In many South American countries provoking a retaliatory foul, with the intention of getting the culprit sent off, is almost an art form. The South American footballer is well tutored in feigned injury and innocent pleading.

Argentina—yes, them once again—behaved disgracefully in the 1990 World Cup finals in Italy. Much of their football was spiteful and eminently forgettable and in the final against West Germany they had Pedro Monzon and Gustavo Dezotti sent off. These were the first players ever dismissed in the World Cup Final. England, incidentally, beaten semi finalists, won the tournament's Fair Play award.

Having gradually witnessed the erosion of the British domination of the world game—England didn't lose to foreign opposite at Wembley until 1953—the British player in the sixties was now coming to terms with an opponent as good as himself and one who also had an array of cunning and unsavoury tricks in his armoury.

There was nothing cunning about a stiff kick on the shin. Aggression in the British game had traditionally been full bloodied, obvious and, as some of the old Victorians had it, manly. But this new threat from some parts of the world to the standards of behaviour in the game was sly and underhand.

At the time the Football Association took great pride in the fact that no England player had been sent off. That changed in 1968 when Alan Mullery, of Tottenham, became the first to be dismissed in a full international. England, the world champions, were playing Yugoslavia in Florence in the European Championship semi-finals. Mullery was a hard, uncompromising midfield player, but not a man who was provoked easily. Nonetheless, when Trivic ran his studs up Mullery's legs the England player retaliated, lashing out with his right foot. Although he didn't connect solidly, Trivic gave a pained performance worthy of the Old Vic. Mullery was sent off and Trivic, suddenly recovered, was as ecstatic as is he had scored a goal.

There is no doubt that it is difficult for referees to achieve a uniform interpretation of the rules within their own domestic leagues, especially where bodily contact is involved. It can be no easier when players from foreign countries meet.

The tactical fouls are among the easiest to spot anywhere in the world— the player who sneaks a five yard advantage at a throw in, the defensive wall that refuses to retreat ten yards, the player who ignores the whistle when a free kick is awarded against him and plays the ball away from the scene of the infringement, thus giving his team time to regroup.

But, much harder to evaluate and interpret correctly, are the physical contact fouls. In recent seasons there has been much confusion in the game in Europe regarding the interpretation of the 'professional foul', which is basically a foul that robs a player of a goalscoring opportunity.

In 1990 the International FA Board issued an instruction that read: 'If, in the opinion of the referee, a player who is moving towards his opponents' goal with an obvious opportunity to score a goal is intentionally and physically impeded by unlawful means, i.e. an offence punishable by a free kick (or a penalty kick), thus denying the attacking player's team the aforesaid goal-scoring opportunity, the offending player shall be sent off the field of play for serious foul play in accordance with Law XII(n).'

The key phrase here is 'intentionally and physically impeded.' It is the referee's duty, having witnessed the incident, to decide in a matter of one or two seconds, whether the offender intentionally and physically impeded his opponent. Even some of the most experienced referees were struggling to interpret this directive accurately. Midway through season 1989-90 the FA took unprecedented action against two referees, Graham Pooley of Bishops Stortford, and Mangal Singh, of Bilston, West Midlands, for misinterpreting the law. They were both banned from taking any further part in FA competitions that season.

'One of the criticisms we get from various authorities in football is that the referees are sacrosanct,' explained the FA's chief executive Graham Kelly. 'I'm quite happy for the impression to be created that they have to stay within the guidelines the same as everybody else.'

The rise in the number of televised games in England and the introduction of new FIFA mandates means that referees are under the spotlight more than ever. If they are under pressure, so, inevitably, are the players. In season 1991-92 referees were given a clear mandate which threatened a rash of red cards for goalkeepers. England's FIFA referee Keith Hackett explained: 'We have been instructed that in one against one situations involving the goalkeeper, where a penalty is awarded, the law demands the goalkeeper shall be sent off. That is, providing the referee is satisfied the opposing player had an obvious goalscoring opportunity.'

The rule didn't change, just the interpretation. In the past a penalty award against a goalkeeper for bringing down an opponent in the penalty area was sufficient punishment. Under the new interpretation, however much the goalkeeper protests, if the referee awards a penalty it means a red card.

In April 1991 the Duke of Edinburgh called together some 30 British sports administrators to answer the question: How can the erosion of the values of sportsmanship and fair play be halted? As President of the Central Council of Physical Recreation, as a former international competitor and President of the International Equestrian Federation and as, simply, a sports enthusiast, he was saddened and puzzled by the decline in the behaviour of sportsmen and women.

'In some countries and some sports,' he said 'anything has become permissible as long as you aren't caught. The end justifies the means.'

Football, as a high profile sport that attracts comprehensive media coverage, was represented by Garth Crooks, the one-time Tottenham striker and former Chairman of the Professional Footballers' Association. 'The greatest problem is inconsistency in interpreting the laws from one country to another, from one referee to another.

'Referees and players have grown apart. Fair play has to be promoted avidly. Brian Clough will not allow his team to take liberties on the field, neither will Howard Kendall nor Ron Atkinson. More managers and directors have to take a share of the responsibility for the actions of their players.'

This lack of consistency, particularly in regard to the interpretation of the professional foul, has caused problems and considerable disharmony in the game in recent seasons. There were quite clear indications that, after the dark years of the seventies and eighties, behaviour on the field of play in English Football League matches was improving. In 1970-71 there were just 37 dismissals in Football League matches. By 1982-83 this had risen to 229. But, by 1989-90, this figure had dropped to 187. The following season, though, this had crept back up to 233 players sent off. Much of this increase was because referees were working to a stricter set of guidelines.

Sendings-off and cautions in Football League matches—1971-91

	SENDINGS-OFF	CAUTIONS
1970-71	37	905
1971-72	41	1685
1972-73	82	2320
1973-74	77	2241
1974-75	94	2412
1975-76	100	2519
1976-77	96	2669
1977-78	106	2998
1978-79	117	3266
1979-80	114	3520
1980-81	120	3333
1981-82	147	3821
1982-83	229	3748
1983-84	163	4067
1984-85	174	4101
1985-86	206	4140
1986-87	215	4037
1987-88	210	4001
1988-89	192	3939
1989-90	187	3650
1990-91	233	3551

Maintaining a high degree of discipline is vital in any sport, both on the field of play and off it. One of the facets of top level sport is that it sets the standards for the rest to follow. Churlish behaviour by the big stars of the game is watched by impressionable youngsters on the terraces and on their television screens and often copied. Every disciplinary procedure, whether it covers the conduct of players or regulates the financial affairs of clubs, needs not only to ensure that offenders are duly sanctioned but that such sanctions provide an appropriate deterrent to others. Disciplinary measures also need to demonstrate consistency.

The rapid rise in violence on the field in the early seventies—sendings-off nearly tripled between 1971-76—seriously damaged the image of the game and caused great concern to the FA, who administered disciplinary matters from their offices at Lancaster Gate in London, and the League, who were based at Lytham St. Annes in Lancashire. It was agreed in the summer of 1972 that the FA would retain control of disciplinary matters, but the League would be allowed to introduce their own points system as a deterrent. Previously players punished for misbehaviour on the field, were allowed to appeal to the FA against their sentences. This involved the player, his manager and club officials appearing at FA headquarters. The FA commission was as fair to the players as possible but Ted Croker, the former FA secretary, questioned whether it was right that these cases should take place at all. It seemed contradictory to him that the basis of administering justice on the football field was that the opinion of the referee was final, yet the FA were, in a sense, actually encouraging dissent by allowing players to appeal against the verdict of referees. He felt the FA were contributing to undermining the authority of the referee.

After lengthy negotiations the FA, the League and the players union, the Professional Footballers' Association, reached an agreement to introduce a new system of automatic suspensions.

The changes were probably accelerated by the introduction on television of slow motion action replays, which allowed TV commentators to make their own expert judgements on any unsavoury incident caught by the camera. This, of course, increased to an intolerable level the pressure on referees and, subsequently, players.

The basis of the 1972 agreement, designed to tighten discipline among players, was this:

Any player reaching 12 disciplinary points would be suspended automatically for two matches. (Previously suspensions had covered a time period and clubs could appeal, hoping to free their players to appear in important games).

A player sent off would miss three matches. (After the first year the suspension periods were changed to one match for 12 points and two matches for a sending off).

The cautionable offences varied from one point for a goalkeeper illegally marking the pitch to four points for continual dissent, fouling from behind or deliberate tripping.

The system, with a few variations, has lasted successfully until today. Now the most common cases heard in person by the FA at Lancaster Gate concern the law that covers bringing the game into disrepute, a rule that caters for practically every contingency not specifically detailed in another form.

Bringing the game into disrepute has become a well-worn phrase in football in recent seasons as the game's authorities have sought to improve the image of the sport before outside agencies, such as the police, see fit to involve themselves on a regular basis. It is not just players who have suffered the wrath of the FA. Brian Clough, one of the best known and most controversial managers in the game, was fined a record £5,000 by the FA in February 1989 for bringing the game into disrepute. He was also banned from sitting on the touchline at League grounds for the remainder of that season. His offence? Striking two spectators who invaded the pitch after Forest's Littlewoods Cup tie against Queen's Park Rangers. It was an incident seen by millions of TV viewers.

Television helps create the climate in which the modern game is played and it is sometimes the reaction of armchair viewers that plays a role in influencing the FA in their decisions. The classic case of this involved Arsenal's Paul Davis who was shown on ITV news throwing a punch at his Southampton opponent Glenn Cockerill. The match referee at Highbury, David Axcell, and his linesmen, missed the incident, but as a result of the TV film the FA fined Davis £3,000 and banned him for nine games.

Clough and Davis both had exemplary disciplinary records but there are players, and the FA are of course aware of them, who glory in hard-man images and reputations for rough house tactics. The Portsmouth midfield player Mick Kennedy was fined £3,000, with a further £2,000 suspended for two years, for newspaper articles claiming he was the hardest man in football and proud of his reputation.

In December 1988 Mark Dennis, a much-travelled player then with Queen's Park Rangers, was fined £1,000 following his 12th sending-off in 10 years in a reserve match. In the same year nine Wimbledon players were each fined £750 for dropping their shorts at a testimonial match two days after winning the FA Cup and, a few months later, Wimbledon's John Fashanu was fined £2,000 and given a three match ban following an ugly incident involving Manchester United's Viv Anderson at the end of a Littlewoods Cup tie. Anderson was given a one match suspension.

But, by far the more worrying development in the game recently has been the spate of mass brawls involving several players. In November 1989 Arsenal and Norwich players were involved in a bitter 30-second fracas at Highbury, seen on TV in 62 countries. The FA charged both clubs with bringing the game into disrepute, fined Norwich £50,000, Arsenal £20,000 and warned that League points would be deducted as a result of any future misbehaviour on the same scale.

'The decision today sends a clear signal that we are finding clubs and managers responsible for the actions of their players and that is not a responsibility they can escape from easily,' said the FA's chief executive Graham Kelly.

The following month, December 1989, the message had not got home, West Ham and Wimbledon were each fined £20,000 by the FA after a 17-man confrontation during a Littlewoods Cup tie in which the West Ham captain Julian Dicks was sent off and six other players cautioned.

In November 1990 the FA finally stamped down hard. Arsenal and Manchester United were handed unprecedented punishment after a mass confrontation of players at Old Trafford. No fewer than 21 of the 22 players on the field became involved in the brawl. The match had been televised and the FA took the unusual step of accepting video film as evidence. Both clubs had fined the individual players they considered most responsible for the incident but the FA decided to fine each club £50,000. More significantly, they deducted two Championship points from Arsenal—who went on to win the title nevertheless—and one from United.

The ganging-up mentality, increasingly prevalent among players, presented referees with a new set of problems. The self-appointed peacemakers among the players on the field often merely added to the confusion. Alan Robinson, spokesman for the Referees Association, said: 'A referee struggles to take it all in. He might know that number five is striking number ten, but is number four grabbing number seven or just pulling him away. There is so much to assess in the heat of the moment.'

Many viewed the FA punishment of Arsenal and Manchester United as excessive but there is no doubt that an example had to be made, otherwise the discipline of footballers could end up in the civil courts. In Scotland four international players—Terry Butcher, Chris Woods and Graham Roberts of England and Frank McAvennie of Scotland—had already appeared before Glasgow Sheriff's Court pleading not guilty to conducting themselves in a disorderly manner and committing a breach of the peace during a Rangers-Celtic match in October 1987.

Six months later the Swindon Town midfield player Chris Kamara was fined £1,200 and ordered to pay £250 compensation by Shrewsbury magistrates in the first prosecution of a Football League player for committing an assault on the field against a fellow professional. He pleaded guilty to causing grievous bodily harm to Jim Melrose, the Shrewsbury Town striker, 10 seconds after the end of a game which Swindon lost 2-1. Melrose suffered a suppressed cheekbone fracture. Kamara claimed he had been the victim of assault and racial abuse from Melrose.

That incident proved conclusively to the world of football that the professional sportsman is not above the law.

Football cannot live in isolation. The game, like any other sport, reflects society. And that produces two areas of concern for referees: a lessening of respect for authority and a growing willingness, as Maradona showed, to bend the rules for personal gain.

Bearing this in mind, I would argue that the level of sportsmanship in football is no worse than in many other professional sports and the determination of the game's authorities to protest and enhance the image of the game is to be admired.

It may be, of course, that further deterrents are required and, in England, the FA, the Football League, the players union and the referees are already talking about introducing a system whereby clubs lose Championship points, or are expelled from knock-out competitions as a punishment for persistent misbehaviour by their players.

With such a deterrent in place would the burly Bolton Wanderers and England centre forward Nat Lofthouse have barged Manchester United goalkeeper Harry Gregg, who was holding the ball, over the line in the 1958 FA Cup Final and been awarded a goal? I doubt it.

'It was more like grievous bodily harm,' Gregg recalled. Such a thing would not be tolerated in the game today.

TENNIS

Peter Blackman

Fred Perry won three Wimbledon singles titles in the bygone world of honour, integrity and subservience; John McEnroe became the champion three times at the All England Tennis and Croquet Club in the world of the fast buck, player power and administrative madness.

Tennis, during the period when Perry won his first Gentleman's Singles title in 1934 and McEnroe's first success in 1981, has endured a bumpy, rocking, roller coaster ride and there is reason to believe it might well clatter completely off the rails in the next decade.

No less a person that Philippe Chatrier, the former President of the International Tennis Federation, highlighted one danger in his farewell message on June 6, 1991, when he wrote: 'Make no mistake, money is now a cancer in the game. Our game really is in danger of dying from too much of it.'

Spite in tennis and not money in tennis was Perry's problem all those years ago and it was epitomised when he won his first Wimbledon title, beating Australia's J.H. Crawford. He returned to the locker room to find his prize—a necktie—draped across a chair.

The tie was not presented to him, no one said a word to him. The snub hurt Perry, a working class lad from Stockport, but it was no more than he expected in the snobbish atmosphere that existed at major sporting events like tennis and cricket. Put bluntly, Perry was not regarded as a gentleman.

'That was how it was in those days,' Perry recalled as we sat in the sunshine at the French Open championships a few years ago. 'When I turned professional it grew much worse. I became totally persona non grata at Wimbledon and it stayed that way for many years.'

Perry, of course, did finally break down the barriers put up against him and one of his special delights when he visits Wimbledon now is to walk slowly past the bronze statue of him near the main gate. 'I do it every year and, do you know something, I can never resist a wry smile,' he said.

Perry broke the hearts of opponents with his fierce determination to win every point and every tournament he entered, but he cannot recall a single incident during a match to even remotely compare with the mayhem that has scarred tennis in the second half of the century.

'I played hard and I hated to lose,' added Perry. 'I swore under my breath if I made a mistake and occasionally I glared at the umpire if I considered he had made a wrong call. But it never went further and certainly the crowd never became involved.'

Dan Maskell, the authoritative tennis commentator with BBC TV, can still recall the soft, blissful summer days when the men wore long trousers and the ladies wore equally long dresses. 'And of course,' he said, 'the clothes were all white and there were no logos on them.'

Maskell, now in his eighties, first played Davis Cup for Britain in 1929. 'No decision by the umpire was questioned,' he added. 'After a game the players would stand outside at the bar and have a lemonade. It was just very nice and it is very sad the way things have deteriorated.

'I don't long for the old days. Of course, I look back with a certain nostalgia, often regret. But some years ago I realised that one has to be adaptable. The clowns come and go, but the game carries on and I am grateful for that.'

Maskell's colleague at the commentary microphone is John Barrett who was in the British Davis Cup squad for two years in the late 1950s. 'I grew up with the Lew Hoad, Ken Rosewall group,' he said. 'The game was not so high powered and certainly television was not the dominate factor that it is now.

'The players always had a few beers together after their matches and the media were invited as well. We tried just as hard as the players do today, but it all seemed more friendly. It was friendly rivalry, if you like. Then the game went open and the money started to pour in. Suddenly, it all changed.'

Barrett continued: 'In the '60s I can remember some players swearing and throwing their rackets around. Bob Hewitt was known as being fiery, but Jimmy Connors was really the first to give officials major problems on a regular basis. The thing I really objected to was his vulgar gestures.'

Barrett also isolated Ilie Nastase as one of the early troublemakers though I can recall Pancho Gonzales causing trouble at dusk at Wimbledon. 'Nastase was extraordinarily gifted,' added Barrett, 'but he was an extrovert as well and he thought he could be funny at the expense of his opponents.'

Nastase was an odd mixture. Like McEnroe he was one of the most gifted shot makers in the history of the game. His extra talent was his deceptive turn of speed and fluid movement—combinations that took him to two Grand Slam titles in New York and Paris.

Sadly, the Bucharest-born mastro also had a childlike, mischievous streak that was his undoing on too many occasions, particularly towards the end of his career when he repeatedly clashed with authority because of his bad behaviour.

But most of all Nastase was a superb entertainer and these days he is none the worse for his escapades. No doors are bolted against him and he seems happy enough as he guides his motorbike through the traffic in his glorious hometown of Monte Carlo.

Both Maskell and Barrett insisted that the arrival of commercial exploitation in professional tennis created a star system, but no one has successfully offered a compelling reason why champions like McEnroe and Connors also allow themselves to become the bad boys of the sport.

Sadly, McEnroe and Connors will be remembered for their outbursts when tennis fans should only be recalling the days when they became champions; days, in fact, when they won 15 Grand Slam titles between them—seven to McEnroe and eight to Connors.

There is no light and shade about McEnroe. Often at the same tournament he works under two guises: when he is bad he is called Superbrat and when he is good he is called Supermac. If he falls in between he usually plays rubbish tennis and then sulks off home to his wife and family.

There are people around who still insist that the McEnroe legend would not have taken root if officialdom had disqualified him at Wimbledon '81 when he failed to attend the champions' dinner after winning his first title. The All England Club withheld his honourary membership and he countered by delivering his 'pits of the world' speech to Wimbledon referee Fred Hoyles on No 1 court after which he was fined £750.

A year later he made his peace with the All England Club and he was made an honourary member. That did not cool his temper because 12 months later he was involved in ugly scenes with a photographer at the French Open. He abused officials and was fined 3,500 dollars.

For the rest of the '80s McEnroe blew very hot indeed. He was fined after a conflict with Connors and a linesman at the French Open and then came some more ill tempered behaviour during his defeat by Brad Gilbert in the Nabisco Masters in New York.

That tantrum seemed to upset him more than most and he went into temporary retirement. He was then fined and accused of unsportsmanlike behaviour and disqualified from the '87 World Team Cup Final when he walked off court.

But the issue that really did cause a major Establishment fuss happened in 1985 when he delivered a verbal outburst against the wife of a former Queen's Club chairman after she claimed he had played 15 minutes overtime on a court she had booked for a singles match.

He refused to apologise to Sheila Boden who said that McEnroe had launched an 'obscene tirade, you wouldn't want to hear such language in the gutter.' As the new decade approach McEnroe and Queen's Club finally made up. But it was a bad scene.

Whatever arguments the McEnroe backers put forward in his defence the inescapable fact is that he is by far the worst and often obnoxious rule breaker. His track record is horrendous. The worst incident I witnessed came when he represented the United States in the Davis Cup against Sweden in '84.

McEnroe and Connors were branded the Ugly Americans after the match and the US Tennis Association banned McEnroe and made the rest of the players sign a Code of Conduct agreement for the following year's campaign.

Connors, though, saw it this way: 'You know, a lot of people thought there was a controversy with me and McEnroe. There wasn't. I mean we had controversy when we played our matches in tournaments, but I think when we both played on the same team, there was a relationship. We both had the same thing in mind and that was to win the Davis Cup.

'But we lost the Cup and all of a sudden it comes out in the 'papers that Connors and McEnroe were real bad guys . . . they're bad for the country and all this kind of stuff. No one was man enough to come to either of us and say it. It rubbed me the wrong way to the point where I kind of lost interest.'

Connors has toned down the grosser parts of his act as he enters the final chapter of his career, but he has no regrets. 'I am proud of all the things I have achieved on a tennis court,' he said. But over the years he has left some wounds that simply refuse to heal.

But McEnroe will always be regarded as the inventor of the Brat Pack. Why did he upset so many people, cause so much hurt among officials who earn peanuts in comparison to the multi-millionaire racket swishers like him? He tried to find an answer in an '87 interview in Esquire.

'The way I am thinking now is this: what satisfaction is there in making someone feel bad, even if you're right? Also, I don't want to go down in history as Nasty Jnr or whatever. When you get to the stage I am now— husband, father, twenty eight years old—the whole thing just gets to sound like sour grapes.

'I don't know. After a while, when I'd get the bad call, what happened next was almost like an addiction. I mean, I'd feel my feet moving toward the chair before I'd even think about going over there. And now I am struck with the rep. I understand that. I might only do something once or twice a match, but that's all people want to remember.

'The thing I hate is that people think it's an act. It's not an act. It never was an act. It's just something that became part of me that I'm trying to recover from because there are more important things to get on with.'

But on a Sunday afternoon at the Australian Open in 1990 McEnroe tripped the aggro wire once again and everyone said that the comeuppance for the lefty from New York had come 10 years too late. But McEnroe hit the destruct button with a vengeance.

The temperatures at Flinders Park, Melbourne, hovered every day in the mid-eighties and McEnroe, like all the other players, liberally greased his face with sun blocker cream and instead of a cap he covered his forehead with a green scarf.

McEnroe looked a slightly silly 30 year old as he prepared to face the Swede Mikael Pernfors in the fourth round; and he looked even sillier as the referee Peter Bellenger and the supervisor Ken Farrar threw him out of the tournament in the full glare of worldwide television coverage.

It was the first disqualification from a Grand Slam tournament in the Open era. Ironically, the net that caught McEnroe was woven not by officials, but by the players who wanted much stricter code of conduct rules and, more specifically, three instead of four steps to a default.

The new rule was instigated by the newly formed Association of Tennis Professionals and the chilling sentence asking McEnroe to leave the stadium was delivered by Britain's Gerry Armstrong, an ATP-employed umpire.

The first set was a deceptively easy 6-1 to McEnroe. He lost the second 4-6, but sealed the third 7-5 despite a warning for intimidating a lineswoman. In the fourth set a combination of situations upset the American.

He began to suffer from the heat, the surface that had become sticky, Pernfors' passing shots and a crying baby high up in the stands. Suddenly, he erupted in his familiar, nasty, old fashioned way.

McEnroe hurled his racket at the court. He then demanded that the referee and supervisor come on court to explain why he was docked a point for racket abuse when the racket was just cracked and not broken. The officials endorsed the umpire's penalty.

With the crowd going wild McEnroe launched himself into a few fatal four-letter words to Farrar. McEnroe could not stop the torent of abuse and finally the supervisor turned to the umpire. 'Send him off,' he told Armstrong.

For years McEnroe had been yelling his signature tune 'You cannot be serious,' at officials. Finally, officialdom struck back. They were now deadly serious and McEnroe looked stunned and his resemblance to a clown with his painted nose and lips, plus his headband that was falling to one side, could not be avoided. Slowly, he packed his rackets away and trudged wearily off the court.

Farrar said afterwards that he had never been spoken to in that way before. Many magazines voted him the Official of the Year for his action that seemed to prove at last that the code of conduct did have teeth. One Australian journalist pointed out that McEnroe had obviously not realised he had taken 'one step too Farrar.'

Later McEnroe was full of remorse, stating that he had forgotten about the rule change. 'I just can't understand what gets into me,' he said. 'The bottom line is that I've let down myself, my family and my friends. That really hurts because I thought I had cracked this problem.'

The serious attempt to crack down hard on the troublemakers who were wrecking the game's image followed one of the most spiteful periods in tennis which, of course, went Open in 1968, allowing professional players to compete with amateurs.

For 15 years the Men's Tennis Council ran men's professional tennis and during its tenure as the governing body the game made significant strides including the development of uniform rules, professional officiating and a drug testing programme.

However, despite these advances, the players felt they needed a greater voice to improve the overall destiny of their sport. In 1988 the players decided to form their own organisation and they invited tournament directors of nearly every major men's professional event to join them as partners in a new opportunity . . . the ATP tour.

That paragraph is contained in the '91 ATP media guide. It conveniently hides months of high drama that started in the car park at Flushing Meadow, New York, during the US Open. It was held there because the United States Tennis Association would not allow them on their stadium premises.

So the media was summoned to a strip of land among the cars and the tennis fans on their way to the US Open. Speeches were made, questions were asked and the future of men's professional tennis was shaped as the smoke from a nearby hamburger stall drifted over the bizarre scene.

Some memorable and fiery arguments followed. All the players were accused of being power hungry and the mega rich stars like Boris Becker and Ivan Lendl were called downright greedy. They were also accused of being lazy as they insisted that if the new tour was successful they would campaign for a schedule that enabled them to play in fewer tournaments.

So often in the past the administrators had complained about the players on-court behaviour, but here they were airing all their dirty linen in public. Finally, the MTC folded. The APT had achieved one of the greatest take-overs in sport, an assertion, incidentally, that was strenuously denied by their first chief executive. Hamilton Jordan.

But there was a sting in the tail. The powerful executive of the four Grand Slam tournaments—the Australian, French and US Opens, plus Wimbledon—coolly announced the formation of a new event, the Grand Slam Cup with breathtaking prizemoney of 6m dollars—2m dollars of it going to the winner who in the first year was the young American, Pete Sampras.

Though the International Tennis Federation deny the allegation, it is widely accepted that the Grand Slam Cup was devised to spite the ATP. Chatrier, in that now famous farewell message, made this point: 'I felt that it was important that there should be a uniform approach by the Grand Slam Committee which, if ever tennis was severely threatened, would be the only means of saving it.'

Tennis was at war during the ATP takeover—and no one should argue with that statement. And the atmosphere became positively bloody when Mike Davies, a former British Davis Cup player, introduced the Grand Slam Cup project in his role as the chief executive of the International Tennis Federation.

Welshman Davies, remembered for organising the first 1m dollar tour— World Championship Tennis—commented: 'We merely returned the ATP's serve. We were being trampled and trampled and trampled on. We needed something. We needed a bit of leverage.

Initially, some players did not welcome the Grand Slam Cup. Becker announced his opposition, while McEnroe, who seldom minces words, was quoted as saying: 'The money is almost disgusting. We are in danger of turning into money whores if we don't turn our backs on things like this, and I might.'

From a purely playing viewpoint it is regrettable that McEnroe and Connors are heading swiftly towards the end of their careers, but even without the duo there is every reason to anticipate that the paid corps of umpires will be kept just as busy during this decade.

One man who used to be a sitting target at matches is David Mercer, though he left the umpiring ranks to become a broadcaster. Mercer, was the top official at the '84 Wimbledon final in which a red hot McEnroe thrashed Connors 6-1, 6-1, 6-2 with some superb tennis.

Mercer has mainly fond memories of his umpiring career though Nastase once shouted at him: 'Umpire, you faggot,' when he awarded a penalty point against him for verbal abuse in a Davis Cup rubber against McEnroe in Bucharest.

'It's no fun being abused by players,' added Mercer. 'But I did have to smile when Connors, after I'd given him a warning for saying 'you stink' to a linesman, asked me whether I'd prefer him to say that the official had a bad odour.'

Even in a world recession there is solid evidence to believe that the huge pile of prizemoney will remain intact with the super rich companies worldwide all eager to climb aboard the bandwagon so long as television's interest is maintained.

That is good news for the young army of performers who are starting to make their mark. Already one or two of them have shown that the old burns marks left on the stage by the likes of Nastase, McEnroe and Connors will not be wiped away completely.

The gangling Yugoslav Goran Ivanisevic, a Wimbledon semi-finalist, Andre Agassi, the multi-coloured act from Las Vegas, Jim Courier, the '91 French Open champion, and the American David Wheaton have already proved that sometimes they can struggle to control their tempers.

Ivanisevic once admitted: 'Well, yes, sometimes I do go a little bit crazy. I do stupid things, but not as much as before.' He was referring to the major scene he created at the European Under-14 championships when, after losing, he smashed his racket, failed to be pacified by his watching mother and was disqualified.

Two years later he was tossed out of a team event in Italy and though he has matured a great deal he still stirs emotions in the crowd. At the '90 Australian Open on the outside courts fights broke out between rival fractions of Yugoslavs in the crowd.

Once when Ivanisevic was given a warning he was asked about the incident. 'Yes, I had a warning,' he answered. 'The umpire should not have given me a warning. I didn't mean to spit in my opponent's direction. I can spit wherever I want. I didn't spit at him, but he was only 10 metres away.'

There is also a high level of humour within Ivanisevic even though he is finding it hard to win key matches. As the frustration built during the '91 season he was asked if he still found it hard to control himself on court.

The powerful left hander who has all the talents to win a Grand Slam, answered: 'No. I can control myself. I just play better when I get a warning, but I don't want a third warning as I will be sent off the court. That's no good, is it?'

Agassi's bark is worse than his bite. His main battles have involved the clothes his wears on court and the men who run the tournaments. Only once has Agassi backed down and that was at Wimbledon '91 when he adhered to the letter to the predominantly all-white ruling.

But 12 months earlier Agassi wore the full range of his technicolour nightmare, which incidentally earns him millions of dollars with the sportswear giant Nike, at the French Open. Chatrier huffed and puffed about the clothes, but basically he did nothing.

When he went back one year later Agassi was asked to comment about a remark by an ATP official who said that he lacked pride in his profession. 'I have just learned not have an opinion about something until I hear it from the horse's mouth,' he said. 'I have said things that people have taken out of context and I don't like that. I have no comment.'

Agassi was also asked if he was trying to change his public image. 'I have to say yes,' he replied. 'It was 100 per cent my decision, realising there was a problem of communication between myself and the public and it concerned me. I felt the need show people a bit more about me.'

Then at Wimbledon '91 Agassi wore white and everything went smoothly until he decided to wear a pair of fancy sunglasses at the start of a match. No rules were broken, the All England Club did not object and Agassi never denied that he made a mint for himself and the manufacturers of the glasses.

Courier is one of a more than useful pack of youngsters who have already moved positively into the playgrounds once patrolled by a long list of great American players. And he is a one off, which is a bonus for the fans. The boy from Dade City, Florida, whose father works in an orange juice factory, wears a white baseball cap, lets his shirt hang outside his shorts, has a variety of mannerisms and gives short, sharp answers at his press conferences.

And he does not mind challenging umpires if he feels something is wrong. Another point about Courier is that he can welcome the support from the crowd one minute—and then suddenly turn on them the next.

When he was asked to explain one moment of conflict with the crowd while beating Stefan Edberg in the quarter finals at the French Open he answered: 'Someone faked a sneeze when I was serving and that annoyed me.

'The truth is that when you're writing your articles I wouldn't think of coming into interrupt you. I call that cheap and it got me fired up a bit. Maybe it was a good thing it happened.'

Wheaton's entry into the Bad Boy class occurred at the first Grand Slam Cup in Munich and, in it's way, it ranked as one of the worst displays of white hot fury because it involved both players. The umpire was a startled bystander.

Wheaton, from Lake Minnetonka, Minneapolis, nearly drowned in a high voltage rage with the old pro Brad Gilbert after a call had been disputed. Gilbert said that someone in Wheaton's group, who was sitting at the side of the court, had shouted something at him.

The pair walked to the net, whacked their rackets on the tape and shouted at each other with only an inch of daylight between their noses. It was an ugly eyeball to eyeball confrontation that forced the match officials, Farrar and Bruno Rebeuh, to rush on court.

The upshot was that the players were fined and the Grand Slam Committee was instantly informed from all quarters that they should not have expected anything else once they chose to stage a tournament with prize money totalling 6m dollars.

The theory is that if the prize money continues to rise at that particular event then there is a high risk that the players, in their frantic end-of-the-year scramble for a slice of the rich cake, will resort to mayhem and disregard the chances of a puny fine.

The quiet Swede Stefan Edberg, who has won Wimbledon and the Australian Open twice each, brought a period of ultra calm to the top of the game when he replaced Lendl as the world No 1. Edberg played a lot, made a fortune and always kept his lip buttoned in the big and small matches.

'The way I see it,' Edberg once said, 'is that I earn my living playing tennis. That's all. No one gives me a cent for climbing on a soap box and arguing a point for myself or anyone else for that matter. What is the point of it all?'

Over the years Edberg has watched the explosions, the tantrums and the warnings take place on the other side of the net. Often, in the heat of a major tiff, he will select a shady spot near the backcourt canvas, rest and smile quietly to himself. All the members of the Brat Pack know that is futile trying to draw Edberg into an argument in an effort to break his concentration or get him riled. The hard fact is that Edberg prefers heat in his right arm and not in his mouth.

After Edberg had beaten McEnroe at Wimbledon '91 he talked briefly about the American's minor altercations with the umpire. 'I know John well enough,' he said. 'I basically expect him to get into a row with the umpire at some stage during a match. That is acceptable. He has got a right to go up there to the umpire and say what he likes. It really doesn't bother me. I just let the umpire handle him. It has got nothing to do with me. There are always going to be a few bad calls on grass.'

Lendl, in many ways, was like Edberg, preferring to let his racket do all the talking during a marathon run as the top player in the world. And though he is still trying to win Wimbledon for the first time he has enjoyed a stupendous career with eight Grand Slam successes and a cupboard packed with other trophies.

An insight into Lendl's thinking with regard to the topic of 'do players hold grudges?' followed his sensational defeat by Michael Chang in the Final of the '89 French Open at a stunned Roland Garros.

'I've heard it said that I now hold a grudge against Michael Chang,' he said. 'Why should I hold a grudge against him just because he beat me. I've beaten more guys than have beaten me.'

Lendl, warming to the subject, added: 'If they hold grudges, that's too funny. You can hold a grudge, then go out on court and get blown away by your opponent before you get the chance to show him you don't like him. Too bad . . .'

Chang, incidentally, is mild mannered off court, but an unsmiling fighter when he is working. He also thinks deeply about tennis, his opponents and his match strategy which included an underarm serve against Lendl in that memorable Final in Paris.

Lendl was highly miffed and at one stage he stood in mid-court with his hands on his hips, giving Chang one of his famous icy stares. But Chang ignored him, having learned along the way that it is suicide to get drawn into short fuse situations.

Chang, who is 5' 8" tall and often overpowered by the big hitters, recalled a match he lost against McEnroe. 'It was one No 1 court.' he said. 'My mistake was that I let him walk on first. The crowd went nuts. Every seat was filled, even the aisles. It was the last match of the day and it was getting dark. I just shrivelled up. I was weird, really. I felt like the guy who was carrying his bags and I lost very quickly. I learned a lot about the game on that day.'

Britain's Andrew Castle almost certainly learned a great deal at the '90 British national championships when he took a Poll Tax banner on court. Castle later described the protest as 'a prank.' But a group of fuming officials at the Lawn Tennis Association fined him, nonetheless.

Women's tennis is virtually scar free, though it might surprise some people to learn that the legendary Suzanne Lenglen, who died in 1938, was involved in two highly controversial incidents.

The first happened in the US Championships in 1921, then she quarrelled with the Wimbledon umpire in 1926—and promptly turned professional. Details about that incident are sketchy, but old timers still recall that it was 'stormy.'

Any mention of Lenglen must include the late Ted Tinling. After he fell under her spell he umpired many of her matches and when she departed from Wimbledon in '26 he was appointed, a year later, as 'callboy' to the championships, acting as liaison officer between players and the Committee.

Tinling became the first and the greatest tennis couturier and he dressed most of the leading women players. The lace edged panties he designed for 'Gorgeous' Gussie Moran in 1949 were a smash hit. But they were ahead of their time and the autocratic Wimbledon Committee hated the resultant welter of publicity.

They did not suffer in silence for long. Tinling was dismissed and he remained persona non grata at the All England Club until his recall in the early '80s. But what did he think of Lenglen?

'She had everything,' he recalled as we sat in the sun of Monte Carlo a few years ago. 'But like all great champions she had an intensity that often got her into trouble. Most of the time an incident was caused by her own impatience with ordinary players.'

Tinling believed that Chris Evert, who burst into tennis in '71, aged 16, with a semi final appearance at the US Open, changed the face of women's tennis with Evonne Goolagong in the early '70s.

'There had been so much bitchiness between players just before then,' he said, 'but these two had a great influence refining women's behaviour. They both had grace, even though their games were different.'

Certainly, a detailed examination of the disciplinary records of the Women's Tennis Association would reveal that there are no Bad Girls to join the Bad Boys. Bitchiness in the locker room is isolated; major disputes in tournaments throughout the world are rare.

Martina Navratilova, who has won the Wimbledon singles title nine times, has known great happiness as a winner. She has also endured torment, anxiety and frustration during the occasional slumps in her distinguished career. I cannot recall her being involved in a major scene.

'I have put so much into turning myself into a champion,' she once said. 'First came the fitness schedules, then came the dieting and the hours and hours of practice. Why take the chance of throwing all that away in an argument.'

Evert took the same view. 'When I thought there was a bad call I'd check, that's all. I discovered early in my career that disputes snap the concentration. It gave the opposition an advantage. The game is difficult enough without all that aggravation.'

The new breed of women's champions more or less take the same view. As the Navratilova-Evert rivalry diminished the baton was passed to Steffi Graf, Monica Seles, Gabriela Sabatini and now the amazing 15 year old Florida schoolgirl Jennifer Capriati.

It would be true to say that the four of them are groomed for fame and fortune on two levels: as performers and celebrities. The more they win, the more they earn through prizemoney; and then high class marketing follows which produces huge payments from endorsement contracts.

The players are warned very early in their blossoming careers that any misbehaviour on the tennis court would seriously damage their image. So, in the main, they become robots: churning out results day after day against moderate opposition and piling up the dollars in the bank.

Seles has strong views about most things. On aggro she said: 'I don't think umpires would be unfair and call the ball wrong on purpose. The point is that you can't change their minds. You just have to accept their decisions. I tend to let those situations go because when you think about it too much you invariably lose the next couple of points. When you are playing in the really big matches the whole idea is to keep the pressure on the opponent, not to give it away because of a disputed bad call.

'I am not saying that bad calls don't affect you. They can disturb you, that's for sure. Some players suffer more than most and you can see their shoulders slump and their eyes get angry. That's when you turn on the heat and try to get the match out of the way.'

Seles was heavily criticised for her non-appearance at Wimbledon '91 and she was later fined after pleading an injury. She was whisked from public view by her friends and backers and her popularity slumped to virtually zero.

The 17 year old Yugoslav ruffled the Establishment feathers when she accused them of discrimination with regard to prizemoney. 'We should get the same as the men in the Grand Slams,' she said. 'The prizemoney is great, but it's only half as good as the men.

'It's unfair. We don't do less. There are not more people watching the men's matches. The TV stations discriminate, too. Jennifer against Gabriela or Steffi against me is as good a match as Forget against Courier, believe me.'

Soon after Seles made those controversial statements some of the Bad Boys were asked for their opinions. All of them thought Seles was talking out of the back of her head. McEnroe, for instance, replied: 'Oh, yeah. Five sets with tie breaks over four or five hours is the same as them, is it. Jesus . . .'

There is spite in tennis and my view is that there always will be, even though we are now in an age when the tough new Code of Conduct has teeth. But I will mourn the day when McEnroe and Connors finally put their rackets away.

And I will regret the demise of the hell raisers. They are rapidly becoming an endangered species. Who can guarantee that the fans will continue to clamour for seats when the sanitised robots of this and the next generation are in action?

McEnroe was exciting, wasn't he? When he was asked about the personal sacrifices he had made he answered: 'Sport, it's so selfish. You can't rely on other people to pull you up when you are not having one of your best days. You don't get the energy from other people.

'So it gets even more and more difficult, and in a way more sacrifices have to be made in order to do what it takes to be No 1 or just to win. It gets so much tougher because your priorities are different. You see the world in a different way.

'You have other interests. You become interested in other things. I have three children I love, a wife that I love. When you are younger sport is your whole life. These days I try to hang back and say 'Wait a minute' there is more to life than all this.'

Just before Chatrier handed over the presidential reins at the ITF he was asked to name the players who have made the greatest impact on tennis during his term of office. He listed Evert and Navratilova, Bjorn Borg—and then John McEnroe.

'Borg's behaviour was impeccable and he achieved the astonishing feat of winning Wimbledon five times in succession, he wrote. 'Then came McEnroe, a superb touch player, whose behaviour was so bad that he was a terrible example.'

Game, set and match, Mr McEnroe.

OTHER SPORTS

Mick Dennis

The qualifying tournament for snooker's Rothmans Grand Prix, at Stoke-on-Trent, is not normally among the highlights of the sporting year. Wannabes and hasbeens, whizzkids and waskids scrap among themselves for the right to play in the real tournament. They are watched by a handful of families and friends and not even the bright posters can lend the place any real glamour.

But when Alex 'Hurricane' Higgins played there in his first competitive snooker match after a one-year suspension it was standing room only in the spectators' area and the hack pack of sports and news reporters and photographers were present in large numbers, craning necks for a vantage point.

Higgins, once the best snooker player in the world and still known by some as the People's Champion, was starting again from the bottom, and although that was sufficient reason for the unprecedented interest in the Stoke event, it is safe to assume that Higgin's unchallenged status as sport's ultimate anti-hero was an additional attraction.

On that tawdry Thursday in Stoke, Higgins chose an interesting ensemble. A physchiatrist could write a thesis on it. The obligatory formal black dinner jacket, which suggested conformity and acquiescence with authority, was set off by a snazzy pair of blue suede shoes which hinted of the old rebellion. The reporters prepared stories likening Higgins to Elvis.

But Higgins's snooker was not as defiant as his footwear. He lost by five quick frames to nil to local lad Adrian Rosa in a match which even the most avid fan could not find really intriguing. There was one interesting moment, however, when the snooker was interrupted by a noisy fan waving a bottle of scotch and shouting the odds. Higgins turned his back on him, disdainful of such unseemly behaviour. Higgins was apparently unaware of the irony that he had frequently been equally boisterous. His own behaviour over the years had seemed just as unsavoury to those who wanted snooker to lose its pubs 'n' clubs image.

Indeed, some of his critics found it astonishing that Higgins was still allowed to play snooker at all. The ban which proceeded his reappearance at Stoke was imposed for a collection of offences which included punching an official and threatening violence against another former world champion, Dennis Taylor. In most walks of life, antecedents like that would have been enough to finish a career, but while many people in snooker were appropriately censorious, it was not difficult to find others eager for Higgins to succeed in his comeback. Higgins, they said, was charismatic and the game needed him. It is an ill wind that blows nobody any good, they protested, and the Hurricane had whipped up considerable revenues for snooker.

On that basis, does the Modern Pentathlon need another Major Boris Onischenko? 'Bent Boris', as he was dubbed by some tabloid newspapers, was the Soviet who gave the sport more publicity at the 1976 Olympic Games in Montreal than it has enjoyed before or since . . . by cheating.

Major Boris, the defending silver medallist, was fencing against Britain's Adrian Parker on the second day of the five-discipline sport when officials became a trifle curious about how well he was doing. The problem was that he didn't actually appear to be fencing very well but the equipment insisted otherwise. The automatic light registered a hit for Onischenko although the bemused Parker was sure he had not been touched.

Then Onischenko came up against Britain's veteran Jim Fox. Onischenko lunged, Fox swayed back and, although the Ukranian's epee clearly did not make contact with any part of his opponent, the light registered another hit. Now it was clear that the epee must be faulty. It was taken away to be examined while Onischenko fenced on with a different weapon (although with noticeably less success). After an hour, the Jury of Appeal announced the stunning news that Onischenko was to be disqualified for 'illegally tampering with his equipment.' Either he or someone acting on his behalf had wired an ingenious, secret circuit-breaker and push-button switch to his sword. By pushing the button he could register a hit whenever he wanted.

The cheating major had already announced that the Montreal Games were to be his last international competition. He was right. Red-faced Soviets whisked him away from the Olympic village and he soon disappeared back into the USSR. He became a caretaker in the Crimea, but since this was in pre-Glasnost days, one can only imagine details of his fate. It is safe to assume that it did not include the sort of popular acclaim which still surrounds Higgins.

Yet it would be surprising if he was not feted by some. It would be surprising if there were not some who raised their vodkas to 'good old Boris'. After all, he had been pretty clever in a sneaky sort of way and had demonstrated the sophistication of Soviet scientific advances.

And he was by no means the first or last Olympian to 'illegally tamper with his equipment.' If you want to talk about equipment which has been tampered with, take a glimpse at weightlifters. Many of them get to look as strange as they do through a combination of stringent, punishing exercise and body-building diet. Others cheat.

Indeed, 12 years before sprinter Ben Johnson was stripped of his world record and a gold medal for using steroids to tamper with his personal equipment at the Seoul Olympics, Poland's Zbigniew Kaczarek did the same and received the same punishment. He set European and Olympic records as he won the lightweight weightlifting, but was then found to have used illegal drugs. In fact, although Johnson's case remains the most infamous instance of the illicit use of drugs, seven other competitors were banned after failing dope tests at the Seoul Olympics, and five of them were weightlifters. But whereas Johnson's case prompted a lengthy public inquiry in Canada and international debate, how many people recall that two Bulgarian lifters, bantameight Mitko Grablev and lightweight Anguelov Guenchev, had their gold medals taken away when they were found to have used a proscribed diuretic (Furosemide) and three other weightlifters were also disqualified? The guilty weightlifters were publicly castigated, of course, but privately it was said by some that they were just unlucky to have been found out.

Unfortunately, we cannot console ourselves with the thought that it is only nasty East European weightlifters who pop pills.

Dean Willey, Britain's Commonwealth Games middleweight gold medallist in 1982 and 1986, was dropped from the squad for the 1990 Commonwealth Games in Auckland after failing a routine drugs test. So the middleweight gold at the Auckland Games went to Welshman Ricky Chaplin . . . who was then found to have excessive traces of the male hormone testosterone in his urine, and was stripped of the title and sent home in disgrace. Another Welsh lifter, Gareth Hives, had to hand back three silver medals after giving a sample which contained traces of the anabolic steroid, Stanozolol.

Three British champions banned and shamed. Shock, horror. The British Amateur Weightlifters Association launched an immediate review of 'drug control procedures both in the past and in the future,' and the applause from around the world was only interrupted briefly by the laughter prompted by the unfortunate comment that 'all urine testing procedures must be water-tight.'

It is no joking matter of course, nor should it be. A head-to-foot guide to the damage which can be caused by steroids, the so-called 'bulk bombs' which help build muscle tissue, makes terrifying reading.

Headaches, insomnia, nose bleeds, heart disease, deformed and underdeveloped bones, liver and kidney disease, infertility, impotence, damaged leg joints and swollen ankles.

That would be enough to put most people off, but it is probable that those who seek to flesh out their dreams by distorting their own flesh are endangering more than their physical health. It is now believed that the drugs which some use to help build their bodies may dismantle their minds. Research by a number of leading American scientists suggests that prolonged use of anabolis steroids can lead to serious psychiatric disorders.

To play Devil's advocate for a moment, however, there is another school of thought. It says that the physique of a successful weightlifter is so grotesquely unnatural, and can only be achieved through such utterly abnormal regimens, that a little bit of extra testosterone hardly makes any difference. Why not let weightlifters do whatever they like to hone their bodies into ludicrous shapes?

And it has to be said that some weightlifters are fairly odd characters, even when their hormone levels have not been illegally tampered with and their minds and bodies have not been artificially altered. Back in 1972, at the ill-fated Munich Olympics, the middle-heavyweight division starred a gentleman called David Rigert, of Chatkhi in the Soviet Union, who was so upset when he failed with three attempts to snatch 160 kilograms that he began to pull out chunks of his hair and bang his head against the wall. He was eventually retrained, with no little difficulty, by a determined group of his hefty team-mates, but he threw another disconcerting tantrum the following day and was sent home.

So the gold went to Bulgarian Andon Nikolov; a former juvenile delinquent who had been introduced to weightlifting at reform school.

Perhaps the most famous weightlifter of all time was Vassily Alexeyev, the massive, jowly, 24-stone super-heavyweight Soviet whose serious-faced picture still adorns the walls of weightrooms and gyms throughout this country and presumably many others. The earth moved when he took the stage and at his intimidating prime he was literally unbeatable. Nobody beat him in competition between 1970 and 1978. He set 80 world records and won the Olympic gold with consummate ease in both 1972 and 1976.

He was once spotted eating a breakfast of a 12-ounce fillet steak and 26 fried eggs. If it is permissible to eat 26 fried eggs, why is a tablet of natural male hormone forbidden? If people are aware of the risks and still want to pop pills before the pump iron, why should we stop them? That is how the argument goes anyway, and I for one would not be prepared to get into a dispute with any weightlifter who feels strongly about it.

While we are being scrupulously fair to weightlifters, let us remember that there are other well-documented cases of Olympians who have illegally tampered with their bodily equipment, or have had it done for them or to them by coaches and team officials. What about all those pre-pubescent girl gymnasts who had their development halted or at least interrupted by the administration of drugs? That surely was far more sinister than grown men choosing to grow a bit more.

Sinister is certainly the correct word for a number of spiteful things that went on in the name of sport behind the Berlin Wall, with women's gymnastics particularly significant and poignant example. It is a sport, after all, which is supposed to be about grace and beauty and yet for many years it was used for blatant political propaganda. The distorted logic was this:

110

success in gymnastics shows that the political system which spawns the winners is itself a winner. To that end, countries were scoured for children (very, very young children) with potential and no trick was missed in ensuring that the potential was fulfiled.

One of the people charged with spotting and developing potential was Renalda Kynsh, a Soviet coach in the town of Grodno in Belorrussia. She was so extremely thorough that she began her talent spotting before possible champions were born. She kept a card index of married couples she thought might produce interesting progeny. One card in her file was marked 'Korbut' and led her, eventually, to an elfin little child called Olga. By the time Olga Korbut was 17 (although she looked about 11) she was bewitching the world with a series of entrancing performances at the 1972 Munich Olympics. The sport mushroomed overnight and it seemed that every little girl who had once wanted to be a ballerina now wanted to be a gymnast.

How ironic that women's gymnastics owes so much of its continued popularity to the cheeky smile of the Munchkin of Munich; a girl-woman who was the product of an intensive factory-farming approach which was the antithesis of true sporting values.

It is equally ironic that the best girl gymnast of all time, Nadia Comaneci, spoke the saddest words ever uttered by an Olympic competitor. At the Montreal Games, after she scored the first perfect 10s in Olympic history, she was asked at a Press Conference what her ambition was.

She said: 'I want to go home.'

Nadia was only 14, but had been selected for special gymnastics training at the age of six. So she had spent eight years being prepared for the Games but when they came, she wanted to be at home. She was still a frightened little girl, and as well as recording perfect gymnastic scores she also provided the most complete example of how lives can be disfigured in the name of sport. The pathos of her comment is only matched by the knowledge that when she did go home to Ceausescu's Rumania, fresh horrors awaited her. The rulers who had already exploited her body continued to abuse it.

And as well as the girls who were robbed of their childhood to satisfy the ugly needs of supposed sports, there were the girls who . . . well, were they girls? The number of allegedly female competitors, particularly in athletics, from Eastern Europe who looked anything but female made them the butt of smutty jokes for the rest of the world.

But, of course, there is no reason why all sportswomen should conform to a stereotype of femininity, and the question of sex tests has become understandably and extremely controversial. Why should women have to prove they are women? The ladies of the British equestrian team at the Seoul Olympics made that point, not altogether flippantly, when they said they would only submit to sex tests if Captain Mark Philips had one too.

111

But although sex tests were first introduced in 1968, the case for them had been established fairly comprehensively 30 years earlier. That was when Dora Ratjen, a German, set a world high jump record of 5ft 7ins. Worried officials were perplexed by her masculine gait and appearance. For the first time in sport the question was asked: 'When is a woman not a woman.'

Whatever the answer, Dora did not qualify. She was told she could no longer compete as a woman, and those who found that an outrageous decision had the wind taken out of their sails more than somewhat when Dora retired from sport to become a waiter called Hermann.

Then there were the Press sisters, Tamara and Irina, from Leningrad. They set 26 athletic records between them and shared a haul of 26 Olympic gold medals. Soviet officials scoffed at questions about the gender of the sisters, but the girls, if indeed that is what they were, retired at precisely the moment that sex tests were introduced (although they always maintained that was a coincidence).

Well-documented cases like those do not make it any less true that the demarcation line between male and female is not easily drawn. A woman who is slight of build and fair of face is not necessarily more feminine than one who isn't and it is grossly unfair to assume that women who are built like brick outhouses are unfeminine. It is not even a simple question of chromosones, because fertility clinics frequently diagnose chromosonal abnormalities without deeming a woman a man.

Nor it is possible to be completely straight-faced about the issue, in fact well-meaning attempts to avoid smirking fail utterly when the events of real life ape a Benny Hill sketch. For instance an Australian man who had a sex change operation began running as a woman and the resultant protests were dealt with by an official called Mr A Batchelor (his real name) who said (honestly) 'It is a pity this thing has arisen.'

But it is not really a humorous subject. It is now quite apparent that some women, particularly but not exclusively East Europeans, blurred the margins of their gender by taking hormones in the pursuit of sporting glory. And a few confused hermaphrodites whose muscular prowess had caught the eye of the unscrupulous talent scouts made a mockery of their sports. Between them they made some events, especially field events involving throwing, a grotesque parody of sport. They turned sport into a freak show.

Yet in the West we had an ambiguous attitude to East European sporting success. We were sanctimonious about gender-bending, we described the use of drugs and the pre-programming of competitors, but we admired the facilities which the old Communist regimes provided. In particular, the phenomenal advance in international sport of East Germany was viewed with envy and suspicion in equal quantities. The success was, according to the party line, an example of the benefits of applied socialism, and although we knew it was actually an example of the benefits of professionalism, performance-enhancing drugs and unrestricted resources, we looked covetously at the smart sports institutes and the free-spending colleges of physical culture.

Nor were we totally opposed to the experiments about which we heard rumours. Was it true that swimmers were given electric shocks to inflate their muscles? Did it work?

When the Berlin Wall was bulldozed, sportsmen and women in the West could hardly contain their enthusiasm. At last we would learn the secrets of the battery Huns. So when an American-based magazine for triathletes published a long article about the secret East German technique of kerb-running (which is not to be confused with kerb-crawling), several Western runners got very excited. Many tried out kerb-running for themselves. The idea was that you ran for a few miles with one foot in the gutter and one on the pavement. Then you ran back along the same route with the other foot in the gutter. It supposedly strengthened your calf muscles, said the article, although there was a clue in the name of the German coach who was quoted extolling the idea . . . Jurgena Hirt. The next issue of the magazine admitted that it had been the subject of a practical joke and that kerb-running was a hoax.

The willing suspense of disbelief by so many runners was a valuable lesson, although I doubt whether many took note of it. The East Germans may not have treated the Games as games, but we are also in danger of taking sport, particularly amateur sport, far too seriously, and of doing almost anything, no matter how dangerous or ludicrous to gain a fractional advantage. Some are prepared to drop into the gutter if it makes them winners.

But if we were ambiguous about our attitude to how the East European sport used people, we were quite clear in our minds about what we thought about what one West German was alleged to be doing to animals.

Paul Schockemohle, the self-made multi-millionaire showjumping rider and trainer, who is the world's largest private horse breeder, retired from international competition on the eve of the 1990 World Championships in Stockholm. A few months earlier German television had shown a video recording which, it was claimed, showed Schockemohle 'rapping' horses at his base at Muhlen, near Bremen.

Rapping, or poling, is the (perfectly legal) practice of hitting a horse's legs with a cane or stick as it jumps. The association of pain with jumping makes the horse jump more carefully and higher. Schockemohle said: 'If it is done in an expert way it is not cruel,' but there was still an outcry, and showjumping, already facing a diminiution of TV interest, lost the backing of some sponsors who were sensitive to public opinion.

113

Then Conrad Homfield, the top American horseman, rode to the defence of Schockemohle and said candidly: 'The rapping issue will certainly get a few backs up, but I'll bet they are the backs of losers.'

And there, finally, we have an honest admission of a view which is central to the debate about sporting spite. A depressingly large number of people in sport share Mr Homfield's cynical view that only losers moan. Some would go further and say that those who harp on about it not mattering whether you win or lose are those who don't win.

And even those of us who disagree cannot afford to be too pompous about people like Higgins, Major Onischenko, Schockemohle and the rest. Because we all like winners, and we are all fascinated by controversial winners. The Evening Standard was represented at Stoke on that Thursday to watch Higgins. We know that he sells newspapers. And although snooker insiders tell me that Steve Davis really *is* very interesting, I don't think I'd drive to Stoke to see him.

But I *have* queued to see John McEnroe, hoping that I might be present during one of his famous tennis tantrums. I know that they are jolly bad form, but given the chance to watch McEnroe or someone like the stiflingly prim Stefan Edberg, I know who I would choose. Edberg? You cannot be serious.

The truth is that the good guys are boring, and the baddies are fascinating. That is human nature, and the principle on which everything from Shakespeare's Othello to BBC television's CrimeWatch is based.

Accepting that fact and understanding it does not mean necessarily that we condone or encourage bad behaviour. Reading Othello doesn't necessarily make one want to kill one's wife, and watching CrimeWatch does not make everyone want to pull a stocking over his head and rob a building society.

But that is where sport differs from many other forms of entertainment, because sport's baddies do encourage emulation. Of that I have no doubt, but I cannot prove it any more than those who disagree can disprove it.

While some sages reason that the decline in standards of behaviour in sport merely mirror similar declines in society, I believe that sporting spite has helped make ours a more spiteful society.

It is, of course, a chicken and egg argument, and the Duke of Edinburgh is among those on the side of the chicken. He has said that the permissive society is to blame for the rise of cheating and violence in sport. He may be right, but I believe that a permissive attitude in sport has led to the rise of cheating, ill-temper and violence in society.

Let me give a couple of examples.

For an article in the Evening Standard magazine I spent one soccer season taking my two young sons to every League ground in London. This was, of course, an investigative mission entirely provoked by the desire to write an incisive piece, and not at all an excuse for being paid to see

Norwich City on all their visits to the capital, but the only time we experienced any trouble, any of the dreaded hooliganism which still keeps young families away from football, was at a game featuring Norwich. They lost 4-3 at Arsenal in a tense match which finished with an unpleasant melee involving several players from both teams. Punches were aimed and shoves were exchanged but although both clubs were later fined by the Football Association, the fracas was over in a few minutes, and supporters insisted that it had been blown up out of all proportion by the wicked media.

After the game, as I nosed my car along a crowded road near the ground, a mob of Arsenal supporters rampaged down the street in hot pursuit of rival fans. They banged on cars and pounded along in the road, their faces ugly with anger. We hid our Norwich scarves, whistled 'Good Old Arsenal,' and sat tight while the disturbance washed past us. My younger son was six at the time, had seen nothing like it before, and needed persuading that it was safe for us to continue our journey.

I cannot prove that the skirmish by the players encouraged the outbreak of unfettered emotion by the supporters, and I was taken to task by Norwich fans for suggesting so in print, but I am happy enough to assert that the fact that the players could not control themselves certainly did not discourage the yobs.

Another example . . .

I coach cub and scout soccer teams and one of my star players of recent seasons has been a little, blond, angelic-faced centre-forward. He was charming boy from a charming, middle-class family. He was diligent at school and polite and pleasant out of school. Except on the soccer pitch.

On the pitch he harangued team-mates, argued with referees at every opportunity, disputed every decision however clear-cut, spat out insults and thought nothing of spitting to clear his tubes, although he would not dream of doing that once the game was over. His hero was Paul 'Gazza' Gascoigne.

Again, I cannot prove that the influence of professional players had perverted him, but again I am confident that regularly seeing top performers abusing officials did not discourage his appallingly disruptive approach to soccer.

And although sport can and still should be a civilising influence, regular involvement with youth soccer teams has proved to me that it can be the opposite only too frequently. One match comes readily to mind. A team of boys was beating another team of boys quite easily, and the manager of the losing team began screaming abuse at his little lads. The abuse got so awful that the manager of the winning team paused from making notes in his dossier to chide his opposite number. But the attitude of the losing manager was supported by parents of his team, who were clearly besides themself with disappointment at the impending result. Some of us who were present

115

found all this a little upsetting at first and then more than a little horrifying, but there was no point in trying to suggest that 'it's only a game.' To the losers it was much more than that.

And the boys involved were all under nine.

What kind of lesson were they learning for later life? And what kind of lesson do they learn from all the cheating which goes on in every sport? You name the sport, and I'll give you an example of cheating.

Sailing? Well, there was the round-the-world yachtsman who hid a little way off Ireland but sent radio messages claiming he was rounding the Horn. Orienteering? Well, there are the allegations of blood-doping; a nasty technique evolved in Scandinavia which involves swapping a competitor's own blood for a transfusion of Oxygen-enriched blood as late as possible before a competition. Mountaineering? Yes there have even been cases of cheating at mountaineering; people claiming to have scaled peaks without actually reaching the summit. American Football? Even college football is riddled with drug-taking, and by no means only so-called recreational drugs. College teams have multi-million dollar budgets, backed by television coverage, and the importance of winning increases in direct proportion to the money at stake, so it is little wonder that some young men choose to seek chemical assistance.

The picture is equally depressing in every sport, and although elsewhere in this book my colleagues come to different conclusions about whether things are getting worse, I believe that in most cases the picture does and will get worse with each passing year. As more money is offered, directly or indirectly, to winners, the more tempting it is to use any means available to avoid being a loser.

What is the solution? How do we make sport less spiteful? If only it were easy to answer these questions, but it is not possible to offer any glib solutions . . . any more than it was possible for reporters to stay away, on that Thursday, from the qualifying tournament for snooker's Rothmans Grand Prix at Stoke-on-Trent.

THE PLAYERS VIEWPOINT

Garth Crooks

As a youth in Staffordshire I dreamed constantly of the day I would don the candy red and white stripes of my local team, Stoke City. Every Saturday my uncle would forsake his West Indian roots—the cover drive off the back foot—and head for his adopted home, the Victoria Ground.

In those days Saturdays represented—for me, at least—all the things that were rich and wholesome in British football, and Saturdays and Stoke City meant Stanley Matthews, a beloved man whose reputation seemed to touch everyone in the area. I can vividly remember my aunt, who watched football under sufferance, talking about the man as though he were a saint, while my uncle, a self-confessed soccer expert, would deign to discuss this one aspect of the game with her. This couple had vastly differing views on many issues but were united by this soccer genius, though it took me some years to appreciate this.

Long before I began to understand the ingredients which won this great hero such status I would wonder why Ferenc Puskas, Alfredo Di Stefano, Lev Yashin and the rest of football's elite would descend on the Potteries on a cold winter night to honour the man. What had he done that was so special? I came to realise that apart from his supreme artistry he had 'played the game' and come to stand for fair play and sportsmanship.

Since those days I have had the good fortune to meet Sir Stan and Lady Matthews. They are a delightful couple who have remained resolute, indeed unmoved, by the helter-skelter changes which have affected the game. Are the pressures so much greater for sportsmen today? Would this unassuming man, who played League football at 50 years of age, still remain aloof from the modern malaise?

During the past twenty years the image of the professional sportsman, particularly soccer players, seems to have been in permanent decline. The process may have been gradual but its effect on practitioners and spectators alike has been dramatic.

Has the sportsman become less sporting? Or has the microscopic attention of the media—which has so expanded in its scope and technology

117

in the period—simply focussed on an historic fact . . . that sportsmen are inherently unsporting! It is a fearful thought, but is it only this opportunity to so analyse sporting spite which has led us to see the low standards we have?

I fondly remember the 1970 Commonwealth Games in Edinburgh when the great Kenyan runner, Kipchoge Keino, lent local hero, Ian Stewart, his favourite running shoes after discovering his arch rival had forgotten his own. Stewart went on to beat the Olympic champion in one of the most thrilling races ever seen in the Games and I recall asking myself the question—'was he mad?' The answer was of course not, but at the age of thirteen I had yet to appreciate how the euphoria of winning should not be allowed to dominate the sporting mind to the exclusion of fair play and reasonableness.

Regrettably, the spirit shown by Keino and the respect earned by Stanley Matthews is much rarer today. The dual dangers of financial reward and the win-at-all-costs attitude have fed off each other like racism off intolerance, growing into some uncontrollable monster refusing to obey its master.

The commercial opportunities available to those intent on being first seem to have not only fractured sporting ethics but seriously damaged the sporting spirit and, furthermore, eroded the often happy division between professional and amateur participants. Now, corporate man has entered many sporting arenas, cheque book to the fore, promising financial security for players, clubs and ruling bodies. Sport is big business around the world; if sport is a business 'product' is must be sold and to be sold it has to be the best, a winner!

The sports star has much to answer for and great influence to exert. As a youngster playing soccer, my love for the game knew no measure but my naivety was similarly limitless and my football youth revolved around copycat performances. I did not realise, until I became a professional player, the impact I and my generation of players was having on the youngsters of the day.

Whilst much blame for the demise in sporting behaviour has been conveniently laid at the doorstep of the sportsman, it should be stressed that managers, coaches and the governing organisations are not without guilt. My induction to the professional game made it abundantly clear that the game was one thing but winning was something quite different. To make the grade I would have to fit myself into the professional framework, the secret laying in how readily I could forget what I had naturally acquired in my formative years and substitute it with the 'winning factor.'

If there is no specific evidence to support the argument that players action on the field directly initiate, for example, hooliganism on the terraces, it can be seen that youngsters emulate their heroes playing styles, gestures and mannerisms. This has both positive and negative results.

118

Amongst the more valuable is the desire to emulate skills, such as Johann Cruyff's famous turn against the Brazilian defender in the 1974 World Cup Finals which, having brought purring admiration from the worldwide television audience, promptly appeared in less perfect form in junior games in every land.

The negative influence is typified by the problem which seems to afflict footballers like no other—spitting. This nasty habit has reached epidemic proportions and is often inadvertently highlighted by a television close-up, usually just as the commentator is reassuring the layman that the player made every attempt to play the ball and not the man. Though youngsters have no physical need to spit, they nonetheless insist on performing the duty with zeal as though to not do so would put them in danger of being less of a player. This shows the effect the professional star has on his public and the need for him to be mindful of this.

The last twenty years has undoubtedly seen a relinquishing of responsibility to maintain the best standards of behaviour, the high profile sportsman becoming indifferent to their rash conduct, submerged by the glamour of top class sport. And yet I am convinced that this decline has been inherited from the game itself. In the days when stalwarts such as Eddie Clamp and Frank Mountford played for Stoke, and on to the ferocious Maurice Setters—who I saw sent off for flattening Denis Law with a headbutt worthy of a fairground wrestler—occasional transgressions never seemed to matter; the game actually respected such players because they were genuinely hard men.

But the eighties saw the situation in danger of getting out of control with bookings, sendings off, spitting and high tackles featuring in every Saturday's reports. Not only were these appalling acts on the increase, their perpetrators were seen to acquire unhealthy kudos from them; they became terrace heroes and media personalities. The game was lauding its louts before praising its artists.

Without condoning the descent of behavioural standards on the pitch, one has to realise the groundswell of deviousness which fosters so many of these negative aspects of the game. Being 'one of the lads' is often a prerequisite for success in a professional sports team and I have seen at first hand how the influence of the other ten can dramatically change the character of an individual. Perhaps it would help if the moderating effect of family life were not treated with such perverse hostility by so many clubs; women are still treated as unwelcome, third class citizens at some soccer clubs who take pride in remaining a bastion of male dominance.

This, added to the environment of intense media hype and partisan rivalry in the crowd, brings problems which are barely recognised by those who badly query why working class lads with truncated educations cannot cope with the pressure of big time soccer.

Why reasonable men—responsible fellows with a wife and children off

119

the pitch—succumb to kicking, spitting and swearing during a game both worries and fascinates me. The well-publicised incident at Old Trafford in October 1990 when Manchester United and Arsenal players 'slugged' it out as the nation watched in horror was an awful sight, though no one actually threw a violent punch in amongst all the pushing and shoving. It was a shocking advert for English football and above all showed an alarming disregard for authority—an endemic affliction of society in general. Over the years I have met most of the players involved and found them intelligent, often charming, and acutely aware of their predicament. So is this the inevitable working out of the stress in the modern game, and is it excusable or acceptable?

Fortunately there have been glimpses of light at the end of this tunnel. Such are the pressures in modern day soccer, the Football Association—the organisation responsible for discipline—has paid particular attention to the behaviour of players on the field, vehemently clamping down on anything remotely suspect. While the action of the ruling body is welcome, it is vital the game itself embraces more of the sporting values exemplified by Gary Mabbutt, the Tottenham Hotspur captain.

It was Gary who, in the 1989-90 season in a game against Aston Villa, instructed his team-mate to throw the ball back to the opposition by way of returning a gesture received from the Villa goalkeeper who had sportingly kicked the ball out of play to allow the Spurs physiotherapist to treat an injured player on the pitch. The order was not only refused by the player concerned later rebuked his captain, stating that the measure was unjustified due to the team's position—with less than 15 minutes to the end of the game, Spurs were training by a goal to nil. Only under a wave of protest did the player later apologise. The salient point here was that the remainder of the team was generally dismayed by the incident and the insubordination but it took a firm stance by Mabbutt to demonstrate this.

If football is genuinely intent on eradicating its problems, managers and directors have to play their part, accept their responsibilities. In no other industry would employees of a multi-million pound concern be permitted to put at risk its image or reputation without the threat of suspension or dismissal.

The way forward was clearly shown by the initiative of Arsenal's Chairman, Peter Hill-Wood when, in 1991, faced with his team's worsening sportsmanship and disciplinary record, he 'read the riot act' to his entire playing staff, manager and coaches included. He promised changes if more self-control was not forthcoming and deserves credit for making his action public.

To the commonly-held stance of managers that 'you have to allow players to let off steam' the question must be asked . . . 'at whose expense?' Furthermore, why should this be necessary for some and not for others; with firmer managerial control behaviour on the field could surely improve. Brian Clough has always insisted his men conduct themselves properly both on and off the pitch and his forthrightness in defence of this has won him admirers. Officials at FA Headquarters are known to have said that Clough's players are 'the ones on time, well mannered and suitably dressed; always good ambassadors of their club.'

There is sufficient evidence to argue that the behaviour of the professional footballer in Britain has improved and certain role models have set good examples. Possibly the most successful striker Britain has produced, Gary Lineker, along with contemporaries such as Peter Beardsley, John Barnes, David O'Leary, Alan Smith, Nigel Clough and Brian Robson are bringing a respectability to the game which recalls the era of Bobby Charlton and Stanley Matthews.

Lineker clearly heads the list. Playing in the most physical of positions, this perfect soccer prototype has captured the imagination of both public and marketeers at a time when being 'good' was in danger of becoming synonymous with boring—a fact of life that snooker star, Steve Davis, has had to contend with.

Unsporting behaviour is not, of course, restricted to soccer. The Olympics, with its original ideals still jealously defended by its organisers, continues to offer an orgy of sporting excellence but does not escape the afflictions of drug abuse, cheating and bad sportsmanship.

When such dramas are seen on television the commentators all too often will add spice to the situation as they consider viewing figures before the best interest of the sport. They will argue they are only offering what the public wants and, in their defence, we are susceptible to scandal, rebels and the good guy/bad guy confrontation. The latter can produce contests, such as Gonzales and Pasarell, Nastase and Borg, McEnroe and Edberg in tennis, which are truly gladiatorial and can leave the spectator physically, mentally and emotionally drained.

Unsporting behaviour has always existed but nostalgia neatly disguises the fact whilst modern media saturation amplifies current examples. Do we all, in a perverse way, enjoy the spectacle and drama of unsporting behaviour? Does it exist to provide the necessary contrast with good sportsmanship? A reflection of daily life. I know the best games I played in had elements of the two extremes yet struck the balance needed to avoid offence.

The welcome calls for radical improvements in sporting standards—facilities and administration as well as behaviour—must be listed to and acted upon without denying or destroying the competitive nature brought about by the will to win.

When I embarked on this piece, nostalgia for the old days came readily. I wonder how much this 'rose-coloured glass syndrome' over-compensates for the magnifying-glass effect of the media on our opinions of the decline in sporting behaviour. These doubts notwithstanding, I suspect the decline

SPORT AND COMMERCIALISM

Caroline Searle

$E = MC^2$. A memorable equation from schooldays. Relative to behaviour in sport it might read: 'Etiquette declines with media interest and commercialisation.' Simplistic? Of course. But whilst it is dangerous to generalise there is a partial grain of truth in this theory—particularly at an Olympic Games where the pressures peak to cause unpredictable behaviour.

There are a myriad obvious exceptions. Gracious sporting millionaires exist alongside offensive cinderellas and vice versa. The contention, though, is that sporting 'black sheep' are a growing breed.

Media and money cannot take the whole blame. Pressure and resulting conflict can occur between individual and team needs; the professional athlete can clash with an amateur administration. Minor differences become glaring discrepancies under the Olympic spotlight.

The Olympic Games is irrefutably one of the world's greatest festivals, for it now transcends mere sport to provide global theatre. Since 1984—and the success of the Los Angeles Games—it has also reached into the realms of big business with major multinationals pumping millions into marketing an association with the Games' perceived traditions and excellence. The ringing of tills is never far beyond the medal rostrum.

Commercial gain is, therefore, not the 'red rag' to the 'bull' of the Olympian code it once was The Charter—every Olympians' book of rules—has not contained the word 'amateur' for two decades or more. Whilst athletes cannot earn money during their sixteen days of glory, they can hear the call of endorsement contracts as the closing ceremony flame dies.

The lucky few—perhaps as little as 2 per cent—will be able to live forever on the colour of their medal. Others will at least be able to cover their costs until the next major event. Money, then, is an undeniable motivation for the modern-day sports competitor. It ranks somewhere on a scale below personal ambition and, sometimes, national pride. But the pressure increases with the potential gains.

And with so much at stake the odd lapse into poor behaviour when expectations are not fulfilled is perhaps understandable. The public, though, is likely to get an unbalanced view as the media focuses on controversy rather than dignity in the face of sporting failure. Athletes are often forced to find transparent excuses and react in anger rather than shoulder the blame themselves.

Athletes from whichever sporting discipline also have an added team, or multi-sport dimension at an Olympic, or other major Games. Therein lies a secondary pressure and potential rub. At current rates it costs between £2 and £3 million to send a British team to the Olympic Games.

Many team members would miss out if they could not rely on overall team funding. Paradoxically, this funding is raised by exclusive contracts with sponsors who may conflict with an individual's backers.

Handled sensibly this need not cause conflict. Frequently, in the Games hothouse, however, the reverse is the case.

Take, for example, Linford Christie at the 1990 Commonwealth Games in Auckland. The London athlete—and eventual gold medallist—came close to being sent home in disgrace before he reached the starting line of the 100m. Sponsored by Puma, Christie appeared to cut off or hide all the Adidas logos on his running kit. And he claimed that his actions were motivated by the needs of comfort whilst racing. Team officials, mindful of the overall team benefit from Adidas, were furious. Both companies secretly revelled in the resultant publicity and a compromise was eventually reached to keep Christie running. But Christie is just one of a new breed of athletes flexing their new-found commercial muscles to buck the system.

Ironically, according to Christie's current contact man at Puma, Derek Ibbotson, such behaviour would have been unthinkable twenty or more years ago. Equally, the pressures would not have been there to warrant such aggression.

In 1956 Ibbotson travelled to Melbourne with the British team for the Olympic Games. 'On arrival', he explained, 'each athlete was given one pair of spikes. That was the limit of commercialism. Nowadays they get, and can lose, so much. They are also full-time athletes which gives them an awful lot of time to dwell on and analyse their performances.'

Ibbotson is convinced that the current pressures to earn a living and the luxury of being a full-time athlete result in selfishness and, at times, poor behaviour. He believes that some athletes become unnaturally obsessed with their preparations so that they live an unbalanced lifestyle.

'That is why Peter Elliott performed so well when he had a part-time job,' claimed Ibbotson. 'He kept things in perspective. We could not afford to buck the system when I was competing. We were totally beholden to the sport's governing body and Olympic team management for sanction to run internationally. They had the power.'

Not that Ibbotson recommends a return to the 'bad old days'. But, like many of his generation, he is also shocked at a loss of values. Requesting money to run for a national team is anathema to the traditional standpoint. Refusing to compete at all in favour of a major money event—just as Monica Seles did where the 1991 tennis Federation Cup was concerned—borders on a criminal offence.

Yet this practice is more widespread in modern sport than might be imagined—and often in the most unexpected quarters. Badminton is usually seen as a middle class sport of mild manners and impeccable etiquette. Yet there is constant friction between some of the top players and their national federations.

The authorities need the star names to play in promoted internationals to fund training and development programmes. Players prefer recuperation and training time between the all-important grand-prix tournaments—the source of valuable pennies and world ranking points.

In such circumstances it is easy for a player to pick up a bad image. And once the rift exists it is more likely to be widened rather than repaired. Altruism sits uneasily with making a living during a necessarily short career.

This is a problem which most sports need to address in a coordinated fashion rather than the current state of haphazard, reactive development. If some form of control and level-headedness is not applied the end result could head towards a chaotic circus. Inevitably this would mean compromise from all sides but could result in a decrease in the pressures caused by new-found commercialism.

'If you put rats in a small cage under the constant scrutiny of hundreds of other rats the decline in behaviour is marked.' The quote comes from an attempt to explain simply the reactions of Olympic athletes under pressure of competition in the media eye.

'Everybody is watching you. You are aware that all the people back home will know, second by second, how well or badly you are doing. It builds up enormous expectation and stress,' said Olympic bronze medallist swimmer Andy Jameson in explanation of the same thing.

The first comparison with rats will be odious to the world's media charged with reporting events to the people. Yet their presence, proximity and numbers intensify the stress on Olympic performers. It is an intensity which affects even the 'bit' players. More column inches and broadcast hours are available to sport than ever before. Detailed analysis is all part of the hype. Even the smaller sports on the programme do not escape, particularly if a nation has a medal hope.

Inevitably, there are those who will come undone at the seams under such scrutiny—either quietly or explosively. And the cameras will always be there to pick up and magnify the fault.

Rowing, and in particular the University Boat Race, has always summoned up images of gentlemanly conduct; of Oxbridge and gentility.

In 1991 that picture was momentarily rocked when Rupert Obholzer, in the Oxford boat, was captured by innovative in-boat cameras making two-fingered gestures at his beaten opponents.

No doubt, Obholzer would claim relief of tension after a gruelling race as his excuse. But the new element in the equation was the on-board cameras—a sign that rowing is moving from a pastime to a part-time occupation for its exponents.

Such media intensity is minor compared with that at an Olympic Games. There were more accredited media personnel (15,000) in Seoul for the 1988 Games than athletes with TV networks worldwide, especially in the United States of America, pouring millions of dollars into their coverage. Other news organisations invested heavily in personnel and equipment installation.

For that kind of serious money they expected their pound of flesh. The stars were chased everywhere. 'I've even had to find a backdoor route to the restaurant to get my food,' said one medal prospect annoyed at having to run the media gauntlet between the protected residential zone of the Olympic Village and the restaurant area.

At any Games—in the pool, on the track, range or pitch—the cameras and notebooks are never far away. They add to the pressures of personal expectation experienced by any top class competitor. 'And if you put an organism under pressure its behaviour becomes less and less predictable,' explained British Olympic Association consultant psychologist Brian Miller. 'The Games, of course, can mean the ultimate pressure to achieve.'

Even sports which are largely ignored during the four-year period are suddenly catapulted into the public domain. Normally placid personalities can 'go wild' in the limelight and perform at their worst. Team managers have to become adept at separating such disruptive influences from the rest of their squad. Meanwhile, others take the change in tempo in their stride and channel it to their advantage.

There are always athletes, though, who will refuse all contact with the media. They are immediately painted as surly and, hence, ill-behaved by the very people who want to interview them. It takes a strong personality to react to criticism positively.

Carl Lewis, current world 100m champion, encountered immense media criticism in the years immediately following his four gold medals at the 1984 Los Angeles Olympic Games. He was accused of being aloof, grasping, loud-mouthed and of questionable sexual preferences. Quite a lot to stomach. Lewis could have hidden but instead decided to call his own press conference to question the media over their attitude. They changed very little but Lewis felt greatly relieved at putting his side of the story.

Double Olympic decathlon gold medallist Daley Thompson, however, has never learnt to use the media. His attitude is one of antagonism. 'And that is a shame', says Brian Miller, 'because all athletes can benefit from the media if they are trained in how to handle the situation. It takes away many of the negative influences and reduces the pressure.'

Learning to handle the media is doubly tricky for those sports unaccustomed to the interest. 'It was certainly different for us going into the 1988 Olympic Games as gold medal favourites,' explained former British Olympic hockey team captain Richard Dodds OBE. 'Before that it had just been one or two dedicated hockey journalists and the odd televised tournament.'

'I don't think we handled it badly,' said Dodds. 'But it does create its own pressures. Since our gold medal success the National League has formed in hockey and the number of players sent off during a match has increased. I don't think we were ever paragons of virtue in the past but there seems now to be that little extra pressure. There is greater importance attached to results because of the media interest. It adds an extra dimension to the normal pressure felt by any sportsperson at any level from within to succeed.'

Malcolm Cooper, twice Olympic smallbore rifle champion, is an intense but warm character who reacts irritably to media attention prior to his competition at the Games. 'They do not want to know about us for four years and then we have to react to their wishes. It is the last thing that I want when I am concentrating on winning.'

Cooper overcame those frustrations in 1988 and invited the newspack to one of his training sessions only to be rewarded by a radio reporter who tripped over his favourite rifle and broke the butt. You only had to look at Cooper's face to see the anguish, and you had to admire his self-control as he gritted his teeth and smiled.

Every Olympic or Commonwealth Games athlete for the United Kingdom is expected, meanwhile, to sign a media declaration. Under its terms athletes agree not to give any media interviews without the sanction of their team manager. The rule is there to ensure team privacy. Athletes, in the past, have divulged information on their team-mates in well-paid exclusives. Other inexperienced athletes have unwittingly created scandal with the odd unguarded word to the media.

Some team members see this declaration as an infringement of their personal rights and are reluctant to bend to the common will. This is another sign of 'player power' and there are justifiable arguments on both sides.

But the more serious breach of accepted behaviour comes from those athletes who sell their participation to a news organisation. These athletes refuse to attend general team conferences on the basis that they do not wish any media pressure before they compete but continue to provide copy for their 'exclusive' contact. Perhaps it is the media falling on a sword of their own making in these cases but it all adds to the difficulties of maintaining team discipline. Equally, there is a dilemma for organisers who depend on finance from sponsors interested in precisely this media interest. Again a voice of reason and compromise is needed.

For the very elite sportsmen and women, of course, scrutiny does not end as they leave the stadium. They are celebrities in the Hollywood sense of the word and their private lives do not escape the spotlight.

Perhaps the most riveting example in 1991 of uncontrolled behaviour in the face of such constant pressure was served up by Boris Becker in the Wimbledon men's singles final. Picture a boyish Becker in the 1985 final juggling a ball on his feet in the sunlight; contrast that with the tortured face, spluttering expletives and moaning into his towel at the changeovers six years later. The actions needed no explanatory words.

Purists were outraged at Becker's demeanour. On a human level, though, they should not have failed to sympathise with someone clearly under such duress.

By contrast again, Linford Christie performed a remarkable feat to turn the trauma of adverse allegations of taking doctored ginseng at the 1988 Olympic Games into the triumph of a silver medal in the 4 × 100m relay. Christie, called before the International Olympic Committee medical commission to explain traces of a banned stimulant in his sample after the 100m final, faced 48 hours of a witch-hunt after his call-up was leaked to the press. He could so easily have been destroyed by the media mania but instead channelled the pent-up anger into the right answer on the track. Christie, no doubt, drew on his years of experience of being in the public eye.

Others do not have the benefit of that experience to draw on. They are thrown in cold and for some it destroys their chance of a lifetime. One of the potential equestrian medallists in Seoul was devastated by the public airing through a Sunday newspaper of their partner's alleged extra-marital affair and impending divorce proceedings. Bobsleigh driver Nick Phipps was similarly affected in his 1988 Olympic season.

These, of course, are isolated cases which represent, perhaps ¾ per cent of a 400-strong team. Others focus their Olympic experience positively. Duncan Goodhew is a prime example. 'I was a kid who was dyslexic and had lost his hair,' he explained. I could have gone wild. But swimming gave me some direction and then the Olympic experience changed my life. I could not have done even half of what I do now without the Olympic family.'

Andy Jameson, 100m butterfly bronze medallist in Seoul, is another shining example of impeccable behaviour under the intense pressure of media and public expectation. He swam his event 48 hours after the gold medal triumph of team-mate Adrian Moorhouse in the 100m breast-stroke. His heat time was the fastest and the media already had him taking the gold medal in the final.

But Jameson had 24 hours to wait between heat and final and had to be satisfied with a 'mere' bronze. Yet Jameson was brave enough to face the media and the public back home moments after his disappointment. He gave a series of interviews, was magnanimous to his vanquishers, gave no excuses and only then retired to nurse his disappointment in private.

All too few of today's champions can step back from the hype to address defeat with equanimity.

It is easy to focus, too, on the controversial rather than the conformist where an Olympic team is concerned. Certainly, media coverage creates that image with the public.

Athletes who reject the team flights, Village food, team accommodation and joint medical services always grab the headlines. Yet the vast majority of Olympians accept the rules and keep their preparations within them. What is more, they will keep the peace at night in the Village when their competition is over.

They are supportive of each other and form a tight fighting unit which feeds off any medal success in the camp. In this sense, Adrian Moorhouse's gold in the opening days of the Seoul Olympics was vital to overall British performances; in contract the Canadians were devastated by the Ben Jonson drugs scandal.

Team-work involves supporting the overall sponsors, sticking to the media rules and accepting the authority of team coaches and doctors alike. Some of the Olympic Village rules are either fundamental human needs or are dictated by logistics. Others depend on the goodwill of the whole team to make them work.

For individual athletes, though, their own preparation, back-up team and methods are considered paramount. Inevitably, conflict occurs with frustrations and misunderstandings leading to poor behaviour and back-biting.

The trend amongst the 'stars' is to reject the system and cause a fuss even if this system helped develop their talent at the beginning of their careers. Many athletes prefer to follow individually-tailored programmes rather than peak for the designated selection trails, another cause of friction.

Often the 'star' happens to be a professional sportsman, the lesser competitor an amateur. The contrast between the two words has often been one of money, but professional can also mean a well-planned approach. Top class sportspeople are professional in the second sense of the word if not always in the first. The search for individual perfection is a constant in elite sport.

Such attention to detail, anticipation and planning is not, unfortunately, always mirrored by the officials who govern some sports. This is sometimes a question of a gap in perception. Sport is still seen by many officials in a Corinthian glow as a hobby which can put them directly into opposition with career-athletes. The resultant lack of chemistry can be explosive and the reaction is more likely to be sparked in the heady atmosphere of an

Olympic Games than anywhere else. Add to the mixture a clash of strong egos and the result can be disastrous.

As sport professionalises its administration such clashes should disappear—particularly if top performers are encouraged to stay with their sport as coaches, officials and administrators.

Faced with the roller-coaster of modern sporting trials and tribulations the delightful French table tennis champion, Jacques Secretin, used to shrug his shoulders in a Gallic gesture and say simply: 'C'est sport.' (That's sport for you).

Whilst attitude and behaviour can be examined microscopically in the light of changed modern pressures it should never be ignored that sport has always strived for the extreme.

Sport, because it is competitive, equals intrinsic pressure. Under that pressure people can behave in a variety of ways—sometimes badly. Bad behaviour is not confined to the elite end of sport. Enter any squash club on a league night and you will see a number of below average performers losing their tempers on court. But such extremes would be the same for any theatre of human activity which involves stress. The elite athlete is more likely to crack because of the additional external pressures.

The way ahead lies in educating athletes to react positively to pressure. They should also be exposed to the Olympic environment well in advance through the media of video recordings and multi-sport competitions. Future progress also involves compromise where conflicting commercial interests prevail. And it demands a greater degree of coordination of world sport.

SPORT AND TELEVISION

Michael Herd

The scene: the women's 3000 metres final at the Olympic Games. The site: Los Angeles Coliseum. The date: 10 August, 1984. Zola Budd of Britain (and South Africa) and Mary Decker of the United States, are the two most famous women athletes in the Western world. Which one will win the Olympic gold medal and a place in history? Half way through a tense and enthralling race, as the pace begins to quicken, the American clips the left leg of Zola Budd as the young Briton, just ahead, moves to the inside lane. Decker pitches forward, tearing the plastic number from Budd's back as she tries to save herself from tumbling to the ground.

The American twists as she falls, lunges over the track side kerb, and screams in her frustration. The scream, echoing round the world on television, is heard in millions of homes. Zola Budd keeps her balance and runs on, the boos of thousands of Americans ringing in her ears, but the will to win has gone. The waif-like runner finishes down the field, is disqualified and, subsequently, reinstated an hour or so later after vehement protests by British officials.

The above incident made for high drama in the stadium and, in particular, on television. Mary Decker was in tears and as she sobbed so she accused Zola Budd of deliberately running too close. For her part, Miss Budd, blood trickling down her left leg, was escorted from the glare of the cameras down the Coliseum tunnel and out of view. It was a matchmaker's dream. There had to be a rematch but where and when? It was inevitable because athletes, promoters and the media are symbiotic creatures. Love or hate does not come into it; simply, they are mutually dependent.

It took the best part of 12 months before the two young women met in competition. The chosen venue was half the world away from Los Angeles. Crystal Palace in South London became the focus of attention as Budd and Decker (who had married British athlete Richard Slaney in the intervening period) prepared to do battle again. The race itself was an anti-climax. Mrs Slaney, as graceful as ever, strode off at the start and was never headed. She won in style with Zola Budd a disappointing fourth. And so the affair might have ended.

Three months later, however, the real story was revealed. And how controversial it was. Andy Norman, promotions officer of the British athletics promotions unit, disclosed that the two runners had been paid nearly £150,000 between them to compete at the Palace. Zola Budd asked for and received £90,000 and Mary Slaney £54,000 ($75,000). Norman explained: 'I asked the Slaney and Budd camps what they wanted. I took these figures to the British TV people and they agreed. I was astonished when the TV people agreed to pay what the two wanted plus an extra £36,000 to assist the promotion.' In fact, television provided a total of £180,000 so that the race could be switched to a Saturday and shown on ABC's Wide World of Sport in the United States.

That event, a rematch of a race that the media claimed had been full of sporting spite, demonstrated as vividly as anything television's influence over sport in the Eighties.

It showed, too, the threat that television poses for the Nineties and into the next century. It is a threat of which television itself is aware. Does it simply report the news or does it also create the news under the guise of entertainment?

Isn't there a risk that by encouraging sporting spite, television is deliberately lowering the standards of sporting behaviour and in doing so incurring the wrath of sport, of sportsmen and women and of administrators?

There was no doubt that the Budd-Decker rerun was an eagerly awaited event but the money television handed over angered many people. Derek Johnson, treasurer of the International Athletes Club, summed it up simply. 'It is an insult to every person in the sport from the greatest athlete to the 15-minute miler and all officials.' Frank Dick, Britain's national director of coaching, said the same thing in a different way. 'It takes your breath away, doesn't it?' At the time, Dick did not need reminding that the fee paid to Zola Budd was just under half the annual national coaching budget, which paid for eight national coaches as well as Dick himself.

With the arrival of satellite channels to challenge the traditional BBC and ITV networks, competition is growing and thus so is the money television is prepared to pay out to invade the privacy of your living room. Dave Hill, the Australian head of BSkyB Sport, makes no apologies. 'Sport is not a requiem mass. It is entertainment. We are story-tellers, the children of the guys who drew figures on cave walls. If you go to a soccer stadium, you see the teams run out and the match. TV gives the viewer a VIP seat. He goes into the dressing room, he hears the thoughts of the players and the coaches, and the commentator should be a knowledgable friend taking him through the match. It is using technology to enlarge the story you are telling. The viewer is now getting more than ever before, and as technology advances, the only limitation a producer has is his imagination.'

Of course, there is always another side to a story and thus television also shows players spitting, kissing, swearing, going over the ball, committing what is described as 'the professional foul', the cynicism that is part and parcel of sport. In other words, is it right that, claiming it is in the public interest, television reveals too often the decline in sporting behaviour? Isn't there another danger, too, and that is that TV creates popularity in sport just as it creates a soap opera (and for the same reasons!). One of the pleasures, explained Hill, is playing out the role of prospector, a gold miner out there in the fields looking to see where the next strike will be. He knows that bowls and darts are popular, that tenpin bowling is growing in popularity but tastes change and nothing is written in stone.

There is overwhelming evidence that television will stop little short of nothing to capture viewers. And if that means controlling sport, so be it! Remember the embarrassing affair of Princess Anne and an American television crew at the Winter Olympics in Sarajevo? The Princess, there as President of the British Olympic Association, was watching Jayne Torvill and Christopher Dean rehearsing to the music of Ravel's Bolero. She was accompanied by the British Ambassador to Yugoslavia, Kenneth Scott, the then Minister for Sport, Neil Mcfarlane (later Sir Neil), Charles Palmer, chairman of the BOA, her personal detective, and her secretary.

A television camera crew from American Broadcasting Companies Inc moved to within four feet of the royal party and focused their camera on the Princess. It was a clear breach of protocol so the detective, a member of Special Branch, stood up and placed his fur hat over the lens of the camera. One of the American crew glowered at the British group and in a voice that carried yards, he snarled: 'Go f*** yourselves. We bought the Games.'

It was difficult to argue with him. After all, ABC had paid $91.5 million for the exclusive television rights in the United Sates. They also had agreed to pay $225 million for the US rights to the Los Angeles Olympics later the same year, and to act as host broadcaster, which involved another $75 million. In other words, for the right to televise the Olympics the American network had paid close to $400 million in six months. I remember Neil Mcfarlane recalling how he had had three thoughts after the confrontation. The first was that the camera crewman had got it right: television had bought the Games. The second was that Lord Killanin, president of the International Olympic Committee, had got it wrong when he had said in Moscow a few years earlier that the Oympics were for the benefit of our children. And the third was that the Games and the world of sport would never be the same again. Television was very firmly in the driving seat.

Television, sets standing in just about every living room in the land, is the most influential of all the media. It took the Gulf War, the Falklands and the Zeebrugge and Heysel Disasters into everyone's home. We were there, prying though a porthole or gazing from a helicopter as it circled over a burning ship. Individual stories of heroism and terror unfolded before our eyes. But was coverage too excessive? Isn't it easy for a camera to become an invasion of grief and privacy? Is there too much violence on television and does it do any harm.

Not unnaturally, that brings us back to sport. Can't accusations levelled at news coverage not also be levelled, on a lesser scale, at sports broadcasts? When we see Paul Gascoigne commit a brutal and stupid foul in a Cup Final televised throughout the world—a classic case of descending sporting behaviour—do we want to view it in replay from three different angles and at several speeds? How many times have we seen Maradona's infamous 'Hand of God' goal which put England out of the World Cup? Do we want to show our children the way in which our sporting heroes behave?

Peter Higgs of the Mail on Sunday related on one occasion how a man had gone into his living room and swore. 'Right there,' Higgs said, 'in front of me, my daughter and the new curtains. He was a footballer appearing in a televised match but he might as well have been one of my neighbours calling round for a cup of sugar. For what he said was real. I couldn't hear the sound but, without any problem, could read the words. They were rude, aggressive and very obvious. So what's to be done? Players and referees must play their part in stopping the foul language and TV directors should be more selective with the close-ups. If they don't the Yob Society will have stormed another citadel—and be living in our homes 24 hours a day.'

There is precious little evidence to suggest that television is selective. The opposite is true. There are overwhelming examples of how television wants to intrude in sport. It wants to move the goalposts and one football club chairman was deluding himself when, at the conclusion of a Football League deal with ITV, he said that the television people might be paying the piper but the League could be pulling the strings. When television companies double and triple the size of their cheques, their measure of control increases in proportion. Wasn't it Joao Havelange, president of FIFA, soccer's world governing body, who suggested that the game should be played in four quarters of 25 minutes to create extra slots for television advertising? In other words, wasn't he approving a television plan to shift the goalposts?

Not long ago there was a vote to decide the presidency of UEFA, the ruling body of European football. The election was between two men, Freddy Rumo and Lennart Johannson. Rumo was a serious-looking, curly haired Swiss lawyer whose duties included the chairmanship of UEFA's Television and Radio Committee. Johannson was a successful Swedish industrialist. The fundamental difference in their stances was that Rumo was and is much concerned about the growing influence of television. He put his name to a declaration that soccer is becoming a weapon in the ratings war between TV stations. That declaration said the game 'should make every attempt to batten down the hatches in the face of this commercial onslaught to protect itself from the deluge of pictures which could ultimately bring about its downfall.' Perhaps it was coincidence that Rumy lost the election.

But does sport have it in itself to batten down the hatches? There are examples that suggest otherwise, particularly from the other side of the Atlantic. We all know that American Football games in the National Football League come to a halt to cater for television advertising, the players waiting for minutes for play to resume. It is the ultimate example of the tail wagging the dog. And what about the case of Tom Kite, the American professional golfer who has won more prize money than any player in the history of the sport. Although golf is a game of self-discipline, the US Professional Golfers Association felt it necessary last year to introduce instant television replays to monitor what they describe as possible rules infractions. The first man to suffer was Kite, winner of the Bobby Jones award for sportsmanship a few years earlier. Kite happens to be one of the most likable, warm-hearted and popular men on the Tour. Everybody loved TK. During the final round of the Byron Nelson Classic, he was penalised a stroke after a television replay, watched by an official in a trailer hundreds of yards away, indicated he might have made an error of judgement. Don't you think that Kite must have felt other players and the public would have perceived that, at the very least, he was trying to take advantage of a situation; a case of sporting spite.

This is what happened. Kite hit his tee shot into a lake demonstrating yet again that golf balls are attracted to water as unerringly as the eye of a middle-aged man to a female bosom. From the tee, it appeared that the hooked, wind-blown shot had passed over a point of land before plunging into the lake. Kite's opponent agreed that Kite was entitled to a penalty drop on that point of land. However, an official, assigned to monitor the television, questioned whether the ball had actually crossed the point of land. If it hadn't—and the official decided that it could not have done so— then Kite would have been required to take his drop on the other, far side of the lake, much further from the hole.

In the end, the American was ordered to play another ball from the tee and finished with a double-bogey six. He went from two shots behind the leaders to four and eventually finished out of the running. He was not amused. 'It's a cop out,' he declared angrily. 'TV made the ruling and I have to live with it. But TV has no business doing what they are doing, making a ruling from an official watching TV in a trailer.' There are many other examples of what many see as unreasonable interference from television. It was only timely action by the Test and County Cricket Board that scuppered a BSkyB screen-it-and-be-damned plan to have former

England captain Mike Gatting wear a microphone on the field in a Sunday League game between his county, Middlesex, and Derbyshire. The plan was for the county captain to be quizzed by commentators Geoff Boycott and Henry Blofeld between overs, with the microphone turned off during actual play. Both counties sanctioned the idea but the TCCB stood firm. 'There have been unfortunate experiences in Australia and New Zealand with microphones in the stumps picking up bad language and players having to rely on someone turning them off at the right moment.'

The satellite channel, clearly warning us about what is to come, have made public their intent to change our perception of television coverage, to give sportsmen and women no place to hide on the field of play. For instance, during live coverage of Sunday League matches, they plan to place micro-cameras inside batsmen's helmets, thus giving us a three-dimensional view of bouncers as they hurtle towards a player's head or chest. 'We may be negotiating some big deals with Test and County Cricket Board so we will keep hammering away at them to change their policy.'

And BSkyB are not alone. Australia's Channel Nine are in the vanguard of what they see as progressive coverage and what many others regard as a contributing factor to a decline in sporting behaviour. Ian Wooldridge, the distinguished columnist of the Daily Mail, described it so: 'Australian viewers hoping to watch Test cricket last week were somewhat alarmed when their screens were suddenly blacked out by a rapidly on-coming meteorite. This, accompanied by a sound-track reminiscent of the Titanic hitting that iceberg, caused old ladies to faint, children to shriek, Vietnam veterans to dive for cover and millions of gallons of the amber nectar to spill over acres of lino.

'When national calm was finally restored it was discovered that what they had see and heard was actually nothing more than a cricket ball striking the wicket of a Pakistani batsman, filmed by a miniature camera embedded in one of the stumps. For their next trick Australia's innovative Channel Nine TV intend to bribe an umpire to pin another tiny camera to the front of his hat so that viewers may have an unimpeded close-up of the adjudicator's right first finger as it imperiously directs a leg-before-wicket victim back to the pavilion.'

Why not go further, Wooldridge wondered. For example, why not insert one of those miniaturised cameras somewhere towards the rear end of Desert Orchid so that we would truly comprehend the psychological problems of horses trying to keep up with him?

In the unhappy event of dear Frank Bruno ever fighting for the world heavyweight title again, why not attach a camera to the sole of his right boxing boot in order to give us a unique view of the ceiling of some Las Vegas gambling dive?

And why not go the whole hog? Why not wire a thumpometer to the chest of an England batsman which would convey the pace of his heart beats to a dial on the small screen as a large and fierce West Indian pounds in to hurl a ball at you at the speed of sound?

What Wooldridge was saying, of course, is that television is only in the infancy of exploiting what it pays sport millions of pounds for. Put another way, can there by any doubts that sport has sold its soul to television?

SPORT AND THE PRESS

Michael Herd

In the space of a few minutes on the sunny afternoon of Saturday, 15 April, 1989, 95 people were killed and more than 400 injured as they watched a game of football. What had been planned as a joyous FA Cup semi-final between Nottingham Forest and Liverpool at the neutral Hillsborough Ground, Sheffield, became Britain's worst sporting disaster, not surprisingly, the Government demanded an immediate inquiry. It was entrusted to Lord Justice Taylor, who acted with admirable promptness. Within a few months he had put forward a series of recommendations that were what one newspaper described as clear, realistic and capable of swift implementation. Those recommendations, well-documented, were designed to prevent a similar occurrence and, thank God, there has been no repeat of the tragedy.

Not long after the disaster, there was another report produced. It came from the Press Council and examined the coverage of Hillsborough by the country's newspapers. It must be said that, by and large, our papers did not emerge with any great credit. It must also be said that what appeared was, in essence, typical of how so many of today's newspapers handle sport. It is worth repeating the Press Council report at length, because the way in which the disaster was handled by our national newspapers produced widespread criticism from the public.

Photographic coverage of the disaster produced a record number of complaints over a single incident. And although the Council, under the chairmanship of Mr Louis Blom-Cooper, QC, received no evidence to identify any particular photographer or journalist as having behaved improperly, it found 'clear evidence' that to people involved in the disaster, some photographers had appeared unhelpful or insensitive. There was serious public criticism of the use of pictures of spectators trapped, injured and dead and of the alleged conduct of some photographers and journalists.

The Press Council found that newspapers were justified in publishing pictures which showed people trapped behind steel fences in distress, pain and fear. It was clear, the Council explained, that serious public interest was served by publication. However, the Council was highly critical of some newspapers for using photographs showing individuals crushed against a fence 'sometimes with features cruelly distorted by its steel mesh,' describing the pictures as 'too gross an intrusion into personal agony and grief.'

Newspapers identified in complaints were the Daily Mail, Daily Express, Daily Mirror, Daily Star, The Daily Telegraph, the Evening Standard, the Guardian, the Independent, the Sun, the Times, Today, the Mail on Sunday, News of the World, the Observer, the People, Sunday Express, Sunday Mirror, Sunday Telegraph and Sunday Times. Few editorial areas escaped uncriticised by the Press Council.

Photographers:

There was serious public concern and anger at the impression that photographers were concentrating on obtaining close-up pictures of those in danger and distress even at the risk of hampering rescue work. The Council conceded that it was the duty of journalists on the scene to record an event without impeding rescue efforts but they and their editors also had another responsibility. They should be aware of the danger that photographers going about their proper work of taking pictures of the injured, dead or distressed may appear callous or insensitive to those involved and by doing so add to their distress. The duty of the editors in the instructions they give and of photographers in the way they behave generally in covering major disasters is to exercise the maximum possible care and understanding for the feelings of all those involved.

Commentaries:

Three examples were the subject of specific criticism by the Council. They were by Edward Pearce in the Sunday Times, Auberon Waugh in The Sunday Telegraph and Richard Littlejohn in the Evening Standard. The Council said that as a point of principle, columnists and observers were free to comment on affairs but that national tragedy or disaster was not an occasion for writers to exercise gratuitous provocation.

The most strongly worded criticism was directed towards The Sun. An article which gave particular offence to readers, including 7000 who signed a Merseyside student organisations petition, occupied the front page of the Sun on 19 April, four days after the tragedy. It was headlined—The Truth. Its subsidiary headline alleged: 'Some fans picked the pockets of victims. Some fans urinated on the brave cops. Some fans beat up P-c giving kiss of life.' The Press Council said the article was unbalanced and its general effect misleading. The headline was insensitive, provocative and unwarranted. The Sun's own ombudsman declared that the article should not have been published in the form in which it appeared. Some while later, the editor of the Sun, Mr Kelvin Mackenzie, agreed that most newspaper coverage of the Hillsborough disaster, including his own, was a mistake. 'It was my decision—and my decision alone—to do that Page One in that way and I made a rather serious error.'

No-one can link a disaster on the scale of Hillsborough with day-to-day sports events but is the reporting and photography topography that much different? It is undeniable that sport mirrors the age so it is true that too many of our newspapers reveal a lack of sensitivity, a lack of judgement and standards, that they are seeking sensationalism rather than the truth. Some editors see themselves as marketing men and the brighter the packing the more units they sell. We have reached the stage where newspapers actively encourage sporting spite and if a decline in sporting behaviour sells a few more papers why should sports editors worry? It is not unreasonable to suggest that sport has been hijacked by television and, to a lesser extent, by newspapers.

It is no coincidence that the papers which most actively seek out sensationalism—and are prepared to pay for it—sell the most copies. They give the punter what he wants. The pace has been set by The Sun and others have followed in a headless stampede. If you want to read a world exclusive 'My Hell by cleared Botham' you buy The Sun. 'I was the most relieved man in Britain yesterday after a judge cleared me of assault. When Judge Richard Hutchinson announced that I was not guilty, I knew that my summer of secret hell was over at last. The allegation that I kicked and punched 20-year-old sailor Steven Isbister hung over me like a shadow all through the cricket season and the Test Matches against Australia . . . I would rather face Dennis Lillee with a stick of rhubarb than go through this again.' If you want to read 'Wild Bothan stripped me naked and covered my body with shaving foam, an exclusive by Geoff Boycott,' you buy The Sun. 'I've been the helpless victim of Guy the Gorilla (Botham's nickname) on more than one occasion. Like in Australia in November, 1979, when he left me in such a state that I was ready to walk into a top hotel wearing nothing but a cap, jacket and my shoes and socks. Botham had stripped me naked on the team coach, soaked me with a water pistol and coated me, from head to foot, in shaving cream.' If you want to read 'You're a Squealer, McMahon' by Vinny Jones you read The Sun. 'I was the man who destroyed Steve McMahon's Wembley dream—and today I label him a squealer with a chip on his shoulder. He has attacked me in his book calling me a big mouth and claiming I didn't worry him in the least when Wimbledon beat Liverpool in the FA Cup Final. But I know just how much I upset him that day.'

Britain's tabloid newspapers, the 'pops', are unique in the world of journalism. They are viewed with bewilderment by foreign reporters and with amazement by the staffs of other, more sober British newspapers. They vie with each other to buy a story, often purchasing an exclusive not to use but to spite the opposition. Their journalists hunt in packs and leave no stone unturned as they unceasingly dig for dirt.

The popular press fuel the hunger of a particular type of reader. But it should be said that the papers themselves are victims of circumstance. It is no coincidence that the arrival of the why-I-eat-goldfish-before-a-big-match type of journalism came at about the same time as players' agent. For a century or so professional sport survived without the services of an agent though they have been compared to carpet baggers. As Neil Wilson of the Independent explained in his book *The Sports Business: the Men and the Money*, professional sport was a feudal peonage and the player little more than a serf in a sporting squirearchy owing his livelihood to the patronage of the lord of his manor. It was they, the entrepreneurs, promoters and club owners, who signed the deals and the players who signed the autographs. On both sides of the Atlantic, the professional player accepted what he was given for the privilege of playing the game he loved, and the owners of ball clubs and arenas closed ranks to exploit him to the full. In England, the Football League prevented players from selling their services to the highest bidder for 75 years by using their monopoly of the professional game to impose a maximum wage. As recently as 1960, the outstanding player in the English game could not be paid more than £20 a week and then only during the playing season. In summer he was paid three pounds less!

All that changed 30 years when the maximum wage was abolished. Since then the rich have become richer (and the poor poorer) aided and abetted by the agent (who, of course, has also become richer). Let me give you an example of the way in which today's stars expect to be paid by newspapers. The Evening Standard's Footballer of the Month is one of the oldest awards in soccer. It has been in existence since before most of today's players were born. The trophy—formerly a cut glass rose bowl, then a silver salver and now a handsome cold cast bronze statue—is treasured by the recipients. They include some of the finest players in the world. Bobby Charlton, Jimmy Greaves, John Charles, Bobby Moore, Denis Law, Pat Jennings, Frank McLintock and a host of others. Since the award was introduced more than a quarter of a century ago, not one player had refused to speak to the Standard's chief soccer writer, formerly the late Bernard Joy (a distinguished centre half with Corinthians, Arsenal and England) and now Michael Hart.

In May, 1990, however, Nigel Martyn, the Crystal Palace goalkeeper advised Hart that he could not be interviewed until the paper had spoken to Eric Hall. Mr Hall was the agent who was running the Crystal Palace players' FA Cup Final pool before their match against Manchester United at Wembley. Some while earlier Mr Hall had rung me and asked if the Standard proposed to make a contribution to the pool. I explained, as I had done to Mr Hall in the past, that it was not the policy of the Evening Standard to make such contributions. On the occasions Arsenal and Wimbledon reached Wembley, the paper had not paid but had been free to talk to players.

Some of Fleet Street's more lurid newspapers do pay. As I have said, buy-ups are the food and drink of agents. But, I asked, why should we pay for the simple right to speak to Nigel Martyn and his team-mates? After all, wasn't it some thing we did quite freely for the other 50 weeks of the years? And in the particular case of Crystal Palace, at every other time in their history. Mr Hall, who by the nature of his job was (and still is) a blunt-speaking person, asked if I was aware of the consequences. As I wrote at the time, I think he meant payee, payee, catchee monkey.

Martyn, who was full of apologies, was not to blame and, upon reflection, neither was the agent. Mr Hall is jolly good at his job. Indeed, he is known as 'Monster, monster' in the business. This, emphatically, has nothing to do with the way in which he is viewed by some people in football. It is because he so describes many of his deals. I suppose, in truth, that the prospering of the agent has had little to do with the player and not much more with the man himself. No, it has lain firstly with injudicious club management and secondly with the papers themselves.

Agents have been called uncomplimentary names by football club chairman and managers. Bobby Gould, then Wimbledon manager, suggested that they are the scourge of modern football. Gould's chairman at Wimbledon, Sam Hammam, described the proliferations of agents as a spread of cancer. But who was to blame in the build-up to the Wimbledon-Liverpool Cup Final when an on-the-pitch photographic session of Gould's players was organised not by the manager or a member of his staff but by Eric Hall. The Professional Footballers Association, the players trade union, have argued that agents are an unnecessary and expensive irrelevance. But down at Selhurst Park, during the Standard's problems with Nigel Martyn, the manager was Steve Coppell. And isn't Mr Coppell a former chairman of the PFA?

Occasionally, the authorities try to fight back. A couple of years ago Paul McGrath, a player with Aston Villa, was fined a record £8500 as the Football Association reaffirmed their determination to clamp down on players writing critical newspaper articles. On the same day Emlyn Hughes, formerly of Liverpool and England, was also found guilty of bringing the game into disrepute. Both McGrath and Hughes had written articles criticising Manchester United and their manager, Alex Ferguson in particular. Ferguson even threatened to take legal action against McGrath.

An FA official said afterwards: 'People must take this as a warning. McGrath has been warned that if he is responsible for a similar article in future, we would consider a suspension. These sorts of articles appearing do not do the reputation of the game any good at all.' McGrath, who had been transferred from Manchester United to Aston Villa a few months earlier, was fined £3500 more than the previous record. That record had been held by a player called Mick Kennedy, who had been fined £5,000 for an article in which he claimed to be one of the League's hardest footballers.

At the time of the offence Emlyn Hughes, former captain of England, winner of 62 caps, was also a director of Second Division Hull City.

There has been another unpleasant development in recent years, typified at the Wimbledon lawn tennis championships each summer, especially during the championship years of John McEnroe. The American, of course, is the personification of sporting spite, a walking example of the decline in sporting behaviour. Each year the All England Club is attended by two quite independent groups of journalists. The first is the tennis writers there to report the serves and vollies, the aces and the agony. The second are known in the business as Rotters. They are news reporters interested only in a story that will move sport from the back to the front of their papers. With McEnroe around, that wasn't difficult.

I recall on one occasion, not with any pride, how I forced him into storming out of a post-match interview by goading him about his conduct. McEnroe — baiting always guaranteed a headline or two. It was common knowledge that interviews with the angry American in the bowels of Wimbledon had an atmosphere like a leaden-green, airless evening before an electrical storm. Asking questions which he found less than inviting could be compared to stepping into a cage at London Zoo and daring to take the temperature of a tiger.

On this particular occasion, McEnroe was playing Andreas Maurer on No. 1 Court. He had broken off serving to snarl at a group of amateur photographers: 'What do you want me to do, pick my nose as well?' After the match, I asked him why he had picked on spectators. I asked him in the certain knowledge that the question would provoke an angry outburst. It did and somewhere along the way, McEnroe confirmed that he thought journalists—and me in particular—were a bunch of 'assholes.' The rotters and I had our headlines.

There was a time, particularly in the case of soccer, when reporters were like public relations officers for clubs, especially in the provinces. Some still are. It is difficult to be uncompromisingly critical of players and officials when one is in day-to-day contact though this has less to do with subornment than with friendliness and, understandably, some professional ingratiation. Somewhere along the way, however, too many of our national newspapers decided that since football is a public property, nourished to a degree unmatched anywhere else and in any other sport by the media, we could obtain from it what we liked, when we liked and for ever how much we liked.

There is no doubt that if newspapers, as a body, decided not to pay for sensationalism we could all get back to reporting sport. I am certain, at the same time, that we would make a positive contribution to stem the declining standards of sportsmanship. All the same, in an age when the agent rules, I have a feeling that some sports, particularly soccer, and some readers, particularly soccer fans, get the newspaper coverage they deserve.

INDEX